DEATH LINES

Death Lines:
Walking London's Horror History
First published by Strange Attractor Press 2023
Text © Lauren Jane Barnett 2023

Cover art by Graham Humphreys
Maps by Natalie Kay-Thatcher
Typeset in **Scala Pro** and Scala Sans Pro
Design/layout by Maïa Gaffney-Hyde

ISBN 9781913689384

Strange Attractor Press
BM SAP, London,
WC1N 3XX, UK
www.strangeattractor.co.uk

Distributed by The MIT Press,
Cambridge, Massachusetts.
And London, England.

Printed and bound in Estonia.

DEATH LINES
WALKING LONDON'S HORROR HISTORY

Lauren Jane Barnett

Maps by
Natalie Kay-Thatcher

For Richard

Contents

Introduction

'I wondered, though, why the best setting in the world for a thriller, a spooky picture, is London in the fog'

– Vincent Price on the set of *Madhouse*, 1974

Much like Dr Jekyll and his sinister counterpart Hyde, Count Dracula and his eternal nemesis Van Helsing, or Sweeney Todd and his steaming meat pies, London and horror cinema share a timeless and irresistible bond. It is a vast metropolis whose streets remain stained with the trace of horrors both real and imagined. This is the city of Newgate and Bedlam, of Jack the Ripper and the Highgate Vampire. The British Museum is said to be the object of an ancient Egyptian curse, and nearly every neighbourhood in the city has its own ghost or poltergeist. In addition to the great Gothic villains above, Dorian Gray took up residence in Mayfair, Sherlock Holmes lived and worked on Baker Street, Alex and his Droogs hung out on the King's Road, and a young Damien wreaked havoc in the London suburbs. For more than a century of cinema, directors and audiences have revelled in the dark shadows cast by London's past and the possibilities this unique city offers for fresh terror.

Since the silent era – with films like *Jekyll and Hyde* (1920), *The Lodger* (1927) and *London After Midnight* (1927) – London has provided a major setting for horror cinema. The H (Horror) certificate was created in 1932 in response to Universal's immensely popular adaptations of Mary Shelley's novel *Frankenstein* (1818) and Bram Stoker's *Dracula* (1897). The first British film awarded an H certificate was Walter Summers' *The Dark Eyes of London*, released in 1939. Since then, more than 140 horror films have been set in London – more than any other British city. Home-grown villains like Jack the Ripper and Sweeney Todd have been reimagined for each decade, but London horror has grown beyond its roots in the neo-Gothic Victorian city. The sixties brought with it psycho killers like the unnerving antagonist of Michael Powell's *Peeping Tom* (1960), or the ghoulish Arthur Pimm in Herbert J. Leder's *It!* (1967). In Harry Davenport's *Xtro* (1982) and Tobe Hooper's *Lifeforce* (1985), aliens were imagined to either infiltrate or destroy the capital of the 1980s. Since the nineties vampires have repopulated the city, and thanks to zombie hits like Danny Boyle's *28 Days Later* (2002) and Edgar Wright's *Shaun of the Dead* (2004), London was to become a defining locale for the millennial zombie resurgence.

Death Lines: Walking London's Horror History emerges from a deep love for, and a fascination with, these films and the city that inspired them. But it also arises from my own experiences walking the city as an occasional horror tour guide. As such, I've planned eight walks – each roughly two hours long – that aim to capture London's many moods and manifestations in horror cinema, alongside the history and myths that have inspired some of the greatest directors. The neighbourhoods and landscapes of the city provide the boundaries for each walk, and the book crosses London from the apparently opulent streets of Chelsea in the west to the cobbled alleyways of the East End. The walks can be taken in any order, and several of them may be connected if you so wish. I've been sure to mark any shared stops, particularly on the London Underground tour, so that you can join the dots in whatever way you like.

Each walk teases out themes shared by the films set in each area, and the ways in which these stories and nightmares respond to the history and character of the neighbourhood. At the end of each walk I've also expanded upon some of these themes by suggesting a series of other locations – or 'horror hotspots' – that you can visit elsewhere in the city. Each hotspot has inspired some of cinema's infamous tales of horror, and most of them appear in several movies. Among these hotspots are two mini-walks, which might take you even further afield into London's eerie hinterlands, to Enfield and to Crouch End – suburbs with deep connections to London horrors, both real and cinematic. Hand drawn maps by Natalie Kay-Thatcher have been provided throughout the book, but you may also want to keep your phone handy.

As you may have guessed, the walks contain a few plot spoilers to offer a vivid picture of each film and the way it uses the city to tell its story. Some you'll probably know, but I hope to introduce you to a few movies you may not have seen. If you come across an unfamiliar tale, the comprehensive filmography provided at the back of the book offers a brief synopsis to help you get the most out of each walk. That being said, a definitive guide to horror cinema in London would run to several thousand pages, so to keep this walking guide portable I've had to leave out many excellent films. This is not, however, a reflection on these films or their differing relationships with London, but an attempt to keep things pointed and concise. Each walk and horror hotspot has been constructed to give a glimpse of London as seen through the lens of horror cinema, refracting the most revisited and reimagined areas and stories in the city.

As I walked the city and wrote this book, I was reminded that cinema did not bring horror into the city but revealed the nightmares that have always lurked restlessly in its subconscious. It is as if the horror has always been here, cloaking the most contemporary serial killers or alien invaders with the same neo-Gothic atmosphere that concealed the actions of Hyde, the Ripper, or Dracula. To walk through London is not merely to pass through this horror, but to live alongside it. This guide is my invitation: horror, walk with me.

Crisis on the King's Road: Chelsea

Walk Length: 2 miles
Starting Point: Sloane Square
Transport: Sloane Square

End Point: Duke of York Square
Transport: Sloane Square Tube
/ Duke of York Square Bus
Stop (G or KP)

What could be less horrific than the King's Road on a sunny afternoon? Lined with glistening glass shopfronts frequented by fashionable clientele, the former private royal road to Kew dazzles with the flash of wealth. Originally a village, but transformed by the residence of Henry VIII (demolished in 1753), Chelsea became a Royal Borough in 1965. Shortly after, the bohemian freedom and youthful optimism of Swinging London redefined Chelsea's character in a collision of old-money elegance and pop-culture icons like Mick Jagger and Mary Quant.

This burst of liberation had its darker side, and the horror films set in Chelsea – eight between 1967 and 1976 – brought the conflicts and tensions of Swinging London vividly to life. On this walk we will encounter the gruesome delight that horror films found in Chelsea's clash of extremes, whether pitting wealthy establishment figures against young nihilistic Satanists, or seeing the same rich conservatives at the mercy of the vengeful poor.

Route

✦ *Starting Point: Sloane Square Station*

A quick glance around the most famous square in Chelsea immediately reveals the beauty and wealth for which the area is known. If you were to take the road going off to the right of the square – Sloane Street – you would soon arrive at the anachronistically cosy green shed of Pont Street Cabmen's Shelter. Since the late 19th century it has offered rest and refreshment for cab drivers on their shifts – a scene recreated in Michael Reeves' *The Sorcerers* (1967). Two cabbies are discussing a newspaper report of a recent murder. One of them recognises a photo of the victim, whom he drove home the night before along with a male companion who must be the murderer. This is a quiet, unsuspecting location for such horrific news, but the location was important for *The Sorcerers*, which was shot predominantly in this area (convenient for one of its stars, Boris Karloff, who lived nearby).

Released shortly before the Summer of Love, *The Sorcerers* is a scorching self-critique directed by an influential filmmaker of the Sixties counterculture who would attain legendary status for directing the better known folk horror classic *Witchfinder General* (1968). The titular sorcerers are two pensioners, Marcus and Estelle Monserrat, who discover a way to manipulate and experience the body of another individual. They decide that the ideal candidate for their experiment is someone seeking 'ecstasy with no consequence' – in other words, one of the young, suggestible, jaded youths who crowd the King's Road. Their thrill-seeking magic takes a dark turn when Estelle becomes increasingly desperate for the sensations that only youth can provide.

In the late sixties and early seventies this bleak vision of voracious pleasure-seeking drew horror directors back to Chelsea again and again. At our next stop we'll have a brush with a character who took *The Sorcerers'* emotional detachment to the level of psychosis.

✦ *Facing Sloane Square, take the road to the left, the King's Road. Continue past Duke of York Square, until you reach another square with a McDonalds on the far side.*

Designed by Anthony Cloughley and modelled after 'Le Drugstore' in Paris, this building was cutting edge architecture when it opened in 1968 as the Chelsea Drugstore. A drugstore in the American sense, this was a place for hip Londoners to shop, have a soda, and hang out.

The Drugstore's trendy reputation and modernist design evidently appealed to Stanley Kubrick, who used it for an early scene in his 1971 dystopian horror *A Clockwork Orange*. Alex, the leader of a violent gang called droogs, has taken the day off school to visit the Drugstore and pick up two beautiful women. His visit is pure psychedelia, shot in the neon-tinted interior of one of the store's record shops. Though the film is set in a dystopian future, the use of this King's Road landmark leads viewers to connect Alex's casual moral depravity with the excesses of Swinging London. Alex is no flower child: by the time he walks into the Drugstore we have seen him brutally beat a homeless man, fight another gang, and rape a woman, usually while high. He is the embodiment of sixties nihilism pushed too far. The film, through Alex's association with the Drugstore, seems to warn against the potential dangers of the emerging counterculture.

Bizarrely, through their fleeting association with the protagonist, Kubrick also appears to take a swipe at the sexually liberated women Alex picks up at this store, one of whom is licking a phallic ice-lolly – a theme explored more prominently in the film at the next stop.

✦ *Continue down the King's Road one block to Wellington Square, just past a flower stall. Number 32 is situated on the right-hand side of the square.*

In Peter Sasdy's *I Don't Want To Be Born* (1975, also titled *The Devil Within Her*) worlds collide in this wealthy, exclusive corner of Chelsea. A newlywed couple – affluent, well-connected Gino and working-class dancer Lucy – bring their new baby back to Gino's home at number 32. Gino thinks he has found happiness with his new family, but we know that Lucy is struggling with a clutch of secrets. She doesn't feel she belongs in Gino's social world; she worries her new baby might be the son of her boss, Tommy, after a long affair that ended only with her wedding; and her baby has been cursed by a man whose sexual advances she rejected. When Lucy claims that the new baby is behaving strangely, even violently, Gino and the family doctor believe she has post-partum depression. We know better: the infant is a demon who nearly drowns his nanny, destroys much of his nursery, and kills his father and, eventually, the sceptical doctor.

I Don't Want To Be Born differentiates itself from other, more famous demon-children films of the era – Roman Polanski's *Rosemary's Baby* (1968) or Richard Donner's *The Omen* (1976) for example – by putting class-consciousness and sexual liberation at the heart of the story. The film heavily implies that Lucy's background, and her attempt to rise into the upper class, lies at the root of her suffering. Once an exotic dancer in a Soho club, she is now a woman of leisure with a lifestyle far beyond that of her former friends – a tension ruthlessly exposed when her demonic child drags the sins of her past into her future. The likelihood that her child is Tommy's son suggests she cannot escape her working-class past, and that her past promiscuity will be her downfall – if not, as the closing scenes suggest, the downfall of humanity.

✦ *Continue along the King's Road another 350 yards until you come upon the Chelsea Potter pub.*

The Chelsea Potter is an institution. Established in 1842 as the Commercial Tavern, it was renamed in 1958 to honour the Chelsea Arts Pottery. A decade later, the pub became a favourite of Jimi Hendrix and The Rolling

Stones, drawing a more bohemian crowd. You can get a sense of this atmosphere in Massimo Dallamano's *Dorian Gray* (1970), in which Dorian returns after nearly a century of travel onto the vivacious King's Road of Swinging London. As if (ironically) overcome by the sight of short skirts and open sexuality he ducks into the pub for shelter.

At this point in the film, Dorian feels isolated: his looks and energy are too young for his former friends, but he cannot find a place for himself among the liberated generation. Cowering in the pub and shaken by the world outside, the final blow comes when the pub TV informs Dorian that the one doctor who may be able to help him age (and die) is dead. The thought of being eternally trapped in a world he sees as rapidly declining is the last straw. He rushes home, grabs a knife and violently attacks his portrait, killing himself. The critique of sixties culture couldn't be clearer: even the most hedonistic man of the Victorian era cannot bear to see the changes happening in Swinging London.

✦ *Continue along the King's Road another 190 yards. Across from the Chelsea Fire Station is a Palladian style Georgian stone house with an iron gate known as 'Argyll House'.*

Argyll House was once the home of the English film director Sir Carol Reed, whose best known works include *The Third Man* (1949) and *Oliver!* (1968). The gothic Victorian atmosphere of *Oliver!* has a long tradition in horror movies, with cramped cobbled streets, gathering fogs, and glowing gas lanterns all adding to a sense of oppressive architectural foreboding. Many of the movies we see in Chelsea were consciously breaking away from this Gothic image in place of a realist horror in an attempt to capture contemporary moods. Resisting this shift however, Hammer Productions, one of the most successful horror producers at the time, continued to stick to this Gothic aesthetic, as we will see at the next stop.

✦ *Continue on the King's Road for about half a mile until you reach Paultons Square on your left. The road is fairly quiet, and you should be able to find a quiet place to stop and take in the square.*

Paultons square is the residence of Lorrimer Van Helsing and his granddaughter, Jessica, in Alan Gibson's *Dracula A.D. 1972* (1972). Here, Jessica turns to her grandfather for help when her friends have raised Dracula from the dead. Van Helsing represents the establishment as a wealthy, respected historian. He also embodies a contemporary link to the Victorian past as he is played by Peter Cushing, who also plays Van Helsing's grandfather, Lawrence, the man who first kills Dracula at the start of the film. His house encapsulates these elements of the past, filled as it is with ancient books, antique furniture, and Lawrence Van Helsing's original notes on Dracula. As the hero of the film, Lorrimer suggests that both the establishment and the past are the places we can look for hope, not Jessica or her young friends; all of whom quickly fall under Dracula's spell.

Although the film is set in Chelsea during London's most swinging period, it presents this new generation as reckless, hapless, and even dangerous. The hipster leader of Jessica's friends is Johnny Alucard (whose last name is 'Dracula' spelled backwards in a nod to the 1943 film, *Son of Dracula*, directed by Robert Siodmak). Alucard not only raises Dracula, but becomes the real villain of the film. Count Dracula gets minimal screen time, leaving Alucard as the primary vampire to seek out victims and convert other members of the group; Dracula merely kills what Alucard brings him. Alucard also represents contemporary fears: when he raises Dracula using a Satanic ritual, the rite gestures towards contemporary fears surrounding occultism in youth culture and stories of esoteric delinquency such as the 1970s Highgate Vampire scandal. This supposedly real vampire lurking in north London was believed by some to be awakened by young people breaking into Highgate Cemetery and dabbling in Satanic practices.

By foregrounding Jessica in the storyline, the film gives a nod to the newly liberated woman, but she quickly becomes the classic damsel in distress, unable to do anything to save herself. With all her friends turned into vampires, Jessica must rely on her grandfather to save the day. It is entirely fitting that the hero of *Dracula A.D. 1972* is an elderly man given that the film was produced by aging horror production company, Hammer, innovators of an earlier age of horror cinema.

Hammer was known for its Gothic horrors based on crudely staged battles between good and evil, a tradition that was perhaps losing popularity by the end of the sixties due to the moral turbulences of an emerging era. The once dominant production company was now struggling against more modern psychological and realist horrors like *The Sorcerers* or, from America, Alfred Hitchcock's *Psycho* (1960). Hammer's insistence on sticking with the gothic style adds an interesting layer to the film. When Van Helsing defeats the much younger Alucard in hand-to-hand combat (see the Holland Park walk), it feels as though Hammer is acting out the fantasy of an establishment stronger than any new wave movement.

✦ *Continue down the King's Road for about 530 feet, crossing over Beaufort Street. Across the road at number 327 is a TriYoga.*

This glass-fronted store beside a brick archway was made into the Cavern coffee shop in *Dracula A.D. 1972*. The young friends, including Jessica and Alucard, meet at the Cavern to socialise. Here, group leader Johnny convinces the group to perform a ritual. Though he lures them in with 'a date with the devil', his true intention is to raise Dracula from the dead. Coffee shops in 1972 were associated with bohemian twentysomethings and university students, often nursing a hangover from the night before. Because of this reputation, the older generations tended to regard coffee shops with concern, viewing their popularity as a sign of laziness and moral decay. With this in mind, when

Jessica is lured to the Cavern by her friends who reveal their fangs before kidnapping her, it vindicated a certain prejudice against young people gathering in these places.

Once kidnapped, Jessica is taken to Dracula at the nearby abandoned church in the World's End district of Chelsea, an area that originally housed a Victorian slum before its later development as a council housing estate. The church was in fact filmed on set but by locating it, and the coffee shop, in the World's End, it sets up a contrast with the leafy townhouse of Paultons Square from our last stop. This part of Chelsea was then – and remains, to some extent, now – a more affordable and less prestigious part of the borough. By placing the young people and Dracula in the poorer World's End and Van Helsing in the wealthier section of the King's Road, the film also touched on the tension of extreme wealth and poverty in Chelsea. Hold onto this idea, because it is central to the film in our next stop.

✦ *Return the way you came along the King's Road and make the first right onto Beaufort Street. At the intersection of Beaufort Street and the Chelsea Embankment, just before the bridge, turn left. Continue 530 feet and turn left onto Old Church Street. Pass the Chelsea Old Church and take the next right onto Justice Walk. Number 7 is no longer numbered but remains as a large black archway next to number 8.*

Moving away from the King's Road, we find horror films focused on the inequality of wealth in Chelsea rather than the risks of the youth movement. The houses of this short, quiet, alley feel almost suburban in comparison with the business of the King's Road. It also exudes a sense of safety that marks cloistered wealth, both of which are undermined in the 1973 horror *Theatre of Blood*, directed by Douglas Hickox.

The film follows the dramatic murders of a series of members of the Theatre Critics Guild, each unsuspectingly attacked as they enjoy their luxurious lifestyles. This black entryway was transformed in the film into the favourite wine shop of critic Oliver Larding. Larding is lured into the cellars below the shop with the promise of a rare vintage, and then captured by a band of vagrants and carried deeper into the cave-like basement while a man dressed in a medieval costume looks on. This mysterious leader begins reading from Shakespeare's *Richard III*, describing a scene where the Duke of Clarence is drowned in a vat of wine. These lines come to life as the vagrants inflict the same fate on the terrified Larding.

The act is one of vengeance. The man dressed in costume is Edward Lionheart, an actor who leapt to his supposed death after his reputation was destroyed by a group of renowned theatre critics – including Larding. Unbeknownst to the critics, Lionheart survived the fall and was washed up by the Thames and nursed back to health by a band of homeless people scavenging along the banks of the river. In secret, he enlisted their help to take his revenge on the critics.

Theatre of Blood revels in the way these affluent people are killed, with each critic dying in a twisted variation of a play they once poorly reviewed. For most of the film, one doesn't even realise Lionheart is masterminding the murders, and so we watch as the visibly down-trodden murder the rich with a ghastly cathartic glee. It isn't quite Jean-Jacques Rousseau's suggestion that 'when the people shall have nothing more to eat, they will eat the rich', but by drowning Larding at his favourite wine shop, he is similarly condemned for his luxurious lifestyle, and his gluttony in enjoying the rarest and most exclusive bottles. There is an almost perverse moral balance to such a murder, an idea echoed in the coming stops.

✦ *Continue down Justice Walk, and you will come out onto Lawrence Street, take a right. Continue along Lawrence Street to Cheyne Walk where you take a left and continue straight until you come to the Albert Bridge. Stop by the statue of a boy and a dolphin over the road from the Bridge.*

This pastel painted bridge is the setting of a brutal beating in Kubrick's *A Clockwork Orange* (1972). After his 'rehabilitation' Alex returns to Chelsea. No longer getting the same thrill from life that he once did, he does not return to his old haunts along the King's Road, instead wandering the Embankment. As he walks under the Albert Bridge, he encounters a clutch of homeless men, one of whom he and his droogs attacked at the beginning of the film. Recognising Alex, the man gathers the group to attack him in revenge. No longer capable of violence, Alex collapses beneath the blows until the police intervene. Unluckily for Alex, the policeman turn out to be two of his former droogs, who takes their own delighted revenge on their fallen leader.

We also see Albert Bridge briefly in Jack Cardiff's sci-fi horror *The Mutations* (1974), where a series of students are kidnapped and have their genes spliced with plants in a monstrous experiment. One such plant-man, Tony, breaks free and wanders London at night where he encounters a homeless man settling down by the stairs beside this bridge. Tony, now enhanced with the instincts and abilities of a carnivorous plant, eats the innocent man. This brief scene is the first time we see Tony attack someone as a mutant, but it is unsettlingly similar to the earlier scene of droogs attacking the homeless man in *A Clockwork Orange*.

In both films, the presence of the homeless touches on the persistent wealth disparity in the borough of Kensington & Chelsea, a dynamic made heartbreakingly vivid following the Grenfell Tower fire of 2017 in which council neglect led to the deaths of 72 tenants. Although these two films do not offer any kind of solution to the social and economic problems that undoubtedly characterise the area, they clearly bring attention to the sentiments of class-based hostility and antagonism that endure, with very real implications, to this day. Fittingly, our next stop will return us to stories of the rich getting their comeuppance.

✦ *Continue along Cheyne Walk, crossing over Oakley street, and stop at number 8. The house has an intricate iron gate in front, and the number is clearly visible above the door.*

Cheyne Walk has long been populated by the wealthy, powerful, and famous – in other words, a perfect place for a little horror. Returning to *Theatre of Blood*, 8 Cheyne Walk is home to another critic, Solomon Psaltery, and his wife. One day, Psaltery receives an anonymous call informing him that his wife is cheating on him. The tipster promises that if Psaltery goes home, he will catch her in the act. As predicted, when he returns to Cheyne Walk, Psaltery spies a young man walking into the house. Psaltery approaches and then sneaks into the house behind the stranger, following him slowly up to the bedroom. Just outside the locked bedroom door, the jealous critic overhears moans and groans coming from his wife. Unable to open the locked door, Psaltery begins screaming. His wife, who happens to be receiving a vigorous massage, tries to calm her husband but the masseur refuses to let her go to the door, pushing her harder into the bed. When Psaltery finally breaks into the room, he pushes aside the masseur in a blind rage and smothers his wife with a pillow. This, of course, mirrors a scene from *Othello*, and as in the play, the wife is entirely innocent, a fact Psaltery does not realise until it is too late. The masseur was actually Lionheart, who used a disguise and the ruse of a massage to set Psaltery up. As with the wine store death of Larding, Psaltery's arrest for murder has a moralistic side, for he committed the deadly sin of wrath – the uncontrolled feeling of rage – as well as envy.

Throughout the film, the rich are killed through their extravagances: Larding dies seeking out an expensive wine while Psaltery's wife is killed for enjoying an at-home massage (a luxury more common today); other critics are killed at hairdressers, at properties they are developing or in their expensive homes. One might be worried that this film finds moral validation in killing the rich, and to a degree it does, but what these displays of wealth truly offer are a suggested motive for the homeless band joining in Lionheart's otherwise very personal revenge. At the heart of the film, Lionheart is unquestionably the villain, chased down by police and ultimately paying the price for his actions.

✦ *At the end of Cheyne Walk, curve slightly right toward the Embankment to a lighted pedestrian crossing on your left. Use the crossing to go east along the Chelsea Embankment. Continue on the Embankment for about 500 yards until you come across an ornate gate to your left with the symbol of Apollo taming the dragon in the centre, topped with a rhinoceros. This is the symbol for the Society of Apothecaries, and once the riverside entrance to the Chelsea Physic Garden.*

Until the mid-19th century the Thames was wider and unembanked, coming nearly up to the pavement, which made this entrance accessible by boat. That is how we see this entry gate to the Chelsea Physic Garden in Jesús Franco's German horror film *Jack The Ripper* (1976), in which the Ripper rows up the Thames to bring pieces of his victims to Flora, a gardener, who disposes of them. At the time the film was set, 1888, this garden was exclusively for use by the society of apothecaries, and only accessible to doctors, medical students, and members of the society. This offers a clue to the identity of the Ripper in the film, as the unique smells of the plants in the apothecary garden allow a blind witness to identify Jack the Ripper as a doctor. At the end of the film, the Ripper is cornered in one of the garden's glass houses – actually filmed on set – and falls to his death. The scene is far more dramatic for the second storey added to the glasshouse, which is not accurate to the garden. But, as you stand outside the back gate, you are standing where the film crew for *Jack the Ripper* did. Having failed to get filming permits for the inside of the Physic Garden, most of the film was made on set but the crew took several establishing shots of the garden through the bars of this gate.

✦ *For the next stop you don't have to walk – just look across the river to Battersea Park.*

Battersea Park, just across the Thames, is the location of choice for fairgrounds in early horror movies. It offers a more convivial mood than Chelsea: not associated with any particular class or social conflicts, the park is a place of unrestricted access and equality. The fairground aspect of the horror films set here offers lights and sounds that spark thoughts of joy, but also create a dramatic backdrop for intense confrontations, turning the uplifting mood of the fair upside-down.

A Battersea Park fair is the glittering evening setting for the climax of Arthur Crabtree's *Horrors of the Black Museum* (1959), which follows a string of murders throughout London using unusual weapons from Scotland Yard's notorious Black Museum, which houses morbid artefacts retained from some of the UK's most significant crimes. At the climax of the film, the young and ambitious Rick takes his girlfriend, Angela, to the funfair. Before this scene Rick is injected with a Jekyll and Hyde type substance by his boss, the crime writer Edmond Bancroft. Though he seems normal at first, Angela notices Rick behaving strangely, and in the Tunnel of Love he goes berserk, stabbing Angela. The police chase Rick up a Ferris Wheel where he confesses that he has killed people throughout London on the instruction of Bancroft. Rick then leaps from the Ferris Wheel, knife in hand, and kills the stunned Bancroft in the crowd below. The pleasure of the funfair is momentarily dampened, but in the final seconds we see the crowd return to the fair and its rides, optimistically suggesting that life always returns to normal.

In a less optimistic horror, Dorkin's London Circus displays its feature attraction – a giant lizard named Gorgo recently captured off the coast of Ireland – at a funfair in Battersea Park in the eponymous *Gorgo* (1961), directed by Eugène Lourié. Unbeknownst to the circus, Gorgo is only a baby whose mother is determined to rescue her child. The rest of the film follows the mother's journey of destruction as she tries to save her child. Despite the best efforts of the electric fence and military presence, the monster demolishes several rides and the circus to save Gorgo, leaving the survivors to watch as the two monsters swim back along the Thames to safety.

The Mutations returns to Battersea Park with a circus sideshow act which appears to be tied to a number of missing students at nearby Imperial College. Early in the film, a female university student is attacked as she walks through the park by Lynch, the menacing, tall, malformed man who manages the sideshow of so-called 'freaks'. His performers are innocent, but Lynch is working for a biology professor at Imperial who is using his students to perform hybrid experiments with plants, such as Tony from the Albert Bridge stop. The freakshow is a clever cover, but when Lynch's murderous cruelty extends to his performers they quickly get revenge.

✦ *Continue along Chelsea Embankment to Tite Street. Turn left and continue on Tite Street until you reach Royal Hospital Road. Turn right on Royal Hospital Road, and then make an immediate left onto Durham Place. This will take you along one edge of Burton Court fields. At the corner of the field turn right onto St Leonard's Terrace. Number 18 is on the left-hand side of the street, and you can see the blue plaque commemorating Bram Stoker's residence here beside the door.*

While the coastal town of Whitby can lay claim to being a huge influence on the writing of *Dracula*, Bram Stoker actually wrote the novel while living in this house in Chelsea. London is also a significant presence in the book, as Dracula buys several homes throughout the city with the intent of converting London's inhabitants into his vampire minions. *Dracula* was made into one of the earliest horror films, F. W. Murnau's *Nosferatu*, in 1922, but the German film received a very limited release because the production never received permission from Stoker's estate. In fact, Stoker's widow would go on to sue the filmmakers. Today the film is well known, and was even remade by Werner Herzog in 1979 as *Nosferatu the Vampyre*. The first officially sanctioned film adaptation of *Dracula* didn't arrive until 1931, when Universal Studios tasked Tod Browning and Karl Freund to film the now famous version of *Dracula* starring Bela Lugosi.

Stopping here it is worth remembering that the tall, dark and handsome vampire played by Christopher Lee in *Dracula A.D. 1972* is not how Stoker would have imagined his Count. This likeness fits better with the alluring image of the undead in John William Polidori's 'The Vampyre', written eighty years before Stoker's book on that famous night when Mary Shelley came up with the plot for her own contribution to the horror imaginary, *Frankenstein* (1818). The image of the vampire in Polidori's story was modelled after his friend, the poet Lord Byron; a far cry from Stoker's image of an old, hunched, long-nosed Dracula. While Polidori's story is not as famous as Stoker's, his image of the tall, dark, and handsome vampire endures in cinema from the 1931 *Dracula* to *Bram Stoker's Dracula* filmed by Francis Ford Coppola here in London in 1992.

✦ *Continue on St Leonard's Terrace until it dead ends.*
Turn left onto Cheltenham Terrace, then right onto the
King's Road. On your right after 200 feet you will find
yourself at Duke of York Square.

We finish this tour of Chelsea's horrors with a reminder
that we have indeed been walking in the past. All of the
films we have encountered in Chelsea were completed
between 1967 and 1976. The brief period in which
Chelsea-set horror films were made suggests that this
area appealed to filmmakers because of its association
with the Swinging Sixties. The social upheaval of the
time offered potential for horror movies by exploiting
the fears that came with change and conflict. Today the
area has settled into a glossy commercialism that could
easily hide any sense of terror the King's Road once had.

As you go, though, do not let this façade fool you.
Chelsea is a place for horror, even beyond the silver
screen. In 1949 John George Haigh was staying at a
nearby hotel when he and a widow guest noticed the
disappearance of a third guest, the elderly Olive Durand-
Deacon. Haigh and the widow went to the Chelsea Police
Station to report her absence, but the police officer on
duty thought Haigh was acting strangely. Brief enquiries
revealed that Haigh had a record of arrests for fraud and
theft. After an hour of questioning Haigh admitted to
killing Durand-Deacon. They had arranged to meet to
discuss his artificial finger-nail business. When Olive
arrived at his workshop, Haigh shot her and then
dissolved her body in an acid bath. Haigh later claimed

that after killing Durand-Deacon he drank a glass of her blood, and that this 'blood lust' had forced him to murder for his vampiric tendencies. Alongside a plea of insanity, Haigh expected to be set free because the acid bath left behind no proof of his admission. Thanks to the forensic work of Keith Simpson however, who managed to identify traces of bodies in the ground by Haigh's workshop, Haigh was found guilty and hanged in August 1949. It may be a far cry from the rites and rituals of *Dracula A.D. 1972*, but Haig is the only known case of a real Chelsea vampire.

Looking for More?

For many horror directors the King's Road offered a visual shorthand to signal Swinging London's burgeoning counter-culture, but it was not the only place horror films did so. In these three horror hotspots we see places throughout London that evoke the same tensions around sex, drugs and youthful rebellion.

Highgate Cemetery

Transport: Archway
Underground Station
(.5 miles)

Waterlow Park Bus Stop HS
(.2 miles)

One of the 'Magnificent Seven' – a series of large, private Victorian cemeteries established in the mid-nineteenth century – Highgate Cemetery exists in two parts: East and West. The East Cemetery, in which notable figures from Karl Marx to George Eliot are buried, is modern and open to the public. On the other side of Swain's Lane lies the West Cemetery, accessible only via guided tours and carefully conserved to capture its visual splendour and unique history. Ivy crawls over headstones and trees, the Egyptian Avenue of tombs looms over visitors, and the famous columbarium and terraced catacombs lend a sense of timelessness and order to the aging cemetery. Stepping into the West Cemetery is stepping into the Gothic.

This aesthetically rich landscape of the dead makes Highgate Cemetery an ideal backdrop for cinematic horror. It appears briefly in films like Freddie Francis' *Tales from the Crypt* (1972) and Terence Fisher's *Frankenstein and the Monster from Hell* (1974) as a quintessential ghostly graveyard, and can still be seen in the backgrounds of horror films today. During the seventies however, horror films were to make the most of contemporary occult interest in this gothic wonderland with such strikingly set films as Peter Sasdy's *Taste the Blood of Dracula* (1970), Andy Milligan's *The Body Beneath* (1970), Robert Fuest's *The Abominable Dr Phibes* (1971) and Freddie Francis' *Son of Dracula* (1974). It is no mistake that three of these films are about vampires, and the fourth, *The Abominable Dr Phibes*, has a fantastic reveal of an empty casket in the cemetery. Highgate Cemetery, in horror and real life, is the home of the undead thanks to the story of the Highgate Vampire.

Though there were a scattering of sightings before and after, the peak of public interest in the Highgate Vampire came between 1969 and 1974. The story – heavily contested at the time and subsequently – revolves around the competing experiences of two men in particular: the languid occult researcher David Farrant, and the more robust self-proclaimed exorcist Sean Manchester. For Farrant the story began in December 1969: he saw a looming spectre in the cemetery and wrote up his experience in the *Hampstead and Highgate Express*. As it turned out, he was not the only one: local papers ran editorials and commentaries by people who also claimed to have witnessed a tall, shadowy figure in and around the cemetery. Farrant initially found the entity more spiritual than vampiric, unlike Manchester, who insisted from the start that a vampire was loose in Highgate.

Manchester's story began slightly earlier in 1967, with a young girl named Elizabeth, who came to him believing she was bitten by a vampire. After a two-year investigation Manchester concluded that the Highgate

Vampire was responsible, and in 1970 made his first sighting in the cemetery. He claimed to have uncovered the vampire's history – a story which, as sceptics pointed out, bore a striking resemblance to the plot of Bram Stoker's *Dracula* – arguing that recent Satanic activities at the cemetery had awakened a centuries-old vampire. Manchester further insisted that he, as a (self-ordained) bishop in the 'Old Catholic Church', should be permitted to perform a public exorcism.

Press interest grew as sightings of the vampire multiplied, culminating in an ITV interview with Farrant and Manchester outside Highgate Cemetery. The broadcast, on Friday 13th of March 1970, included a series of reports of ghost sightings in the cemetery alongside Manchester's detailed instructions on exorcising a vampire. Shortly after the show aired the streets around the cemetery filled with crowds of people – some hoping to join the vampire hunt, but most just wanting to watch – until the police arrived to end the chaos.

Much to the frustration of the Friends of Highgate Cemetery (who see their role as conserving and protecting an atmospheric, historically significant landmark), the legend of the Highgate Vampire has never entirely disappeared, and sightings still occasionally come to light. Not surprisingly, though, its influence on horror cinema peaked in the seventies in the wake of Farrant's and Manchester's sensational accounts. Drawing on a countercultural fascination with the occult, and the moral panic this could provoke, filmmakers focused on the use of the cemetery in Satanic or magical rituals.[1] Many of the films set or shot in Highgate Cemetery include these rituals, especially *Taste the Blood of Dracula* and *Dracula A.D. 1972* (which, though filmed in Chelsea, was strongly influenced by the Highgate Vampire stories). Other films took the concept of the Highgate Vampire head on by putting a vampire in the cemetery.

In *The Body Beneath*, Highgate Cemetery is home to an entire family of vampires, led by the Reverend Ford, for whom the emergent occult interest in the cemetery is, ironically, proving troublesome. The Ford vampires have made their home beneath Highgate Cemetery since Roman times, but in a family meeting towards the end of the film, they decide their cemetery is no longer safe from vandals and thrill-seekers. They leave, though two of the youngest vampires stay on, offering the prospect of a new line of vampires to haunt the cemetery. *The Body Beneath* was filmed before the March 1970 Highgate Vampire ITV broadcast, but, in an instance of life imitating (dark) art, some sightings of the Highgate Vampire coincided with filming in the cemetery.

In a rock-n-roll take on the Highgate Vampire story, *Son of Dracula* centres on the story of the half-human son of Dracula, Count Downe, as he struggles with his destiny as his father's successor. While his coronation

---

1   Poole, W. Scott 'The Vampire that Haunts Highgate: Theological Evil, Hammer Horror, and the Highgate Vampire Panic in Britain 1963-1974' in Kim Paffenroth and John W. Morehead, eds. *The Undead and Theology* (Eugene, OR: Pickwich Publications, 2012) pp. 54-76.

is arranged in London, Downe gets to know the city, visiting Soho and the West End. We only see him feed in Highgate Cemetery in a scene reminiscent of *The Body Beneath*: a young woman with a bouquet of white flowers walks through the cemetery, passing the mossy tombs and the Columbarium. The film places Downe among the stars of London's counterculture – with Ringo Starr as Downe's mentor, Merlin, and Keith Moon and John Bonham as members of Downe's band – but the scenes in Highgate Cemetery remind us that Downe also has a foot in London's past.

Though set in the 1920s, *The Abominable Dr Phibes* reveals the influence of the Highgate Vampire on other kinds of seventies horror. Detectives investigating a series of elaborate murders find themselves at a dead end and follow a hunch to Highgate Cemetery. When they open Dr Phibes' coffin, to their surprise the pristine satin-lined box is empty. Phibes is no vampire, but this wonderfully tense scene echoes the moment in Stoker's novel *Dracula* when Van Helsing discovers that Lucy is not in her coffin. As Stoker's readers already know, Lucy is one of the undead, spreading her vampiric contagion across London. In this film, Phibes is no less deadly, as the coffin reveals he is the killer the police have been searching for.

Soho

Transport: Tottenham Court Road, Piccadilly Circus and Oxford Circus Underground stations all border Soho.

The King's Road may have had Georgian stateliness and aristocratic connections, but Soho embodied a bohemian underworld tinged with sex and sleaze. As mentioned in the Highgate hotspot, *Son of Dracula* exploits this connection, showing Count Downe performing in a Soho club. So does Lindsay Shonteff's *Night After Night After Night* (1969), where the streets of Soho are the haunt of Pete Laver, wrongly suspected of murdering several women he picked up in a club. The police suspect Laver almost exclusively because of his anti-establishment attitude and lifestyle. Similarly, the clubs of Soho are where the young, hip Vampira wants to party in Clive Donner's comedy-horror *Vampira* (1974). Her husband, Count Dracula, is hesitant to let her enjoy Soho as he is shocked to discover how much it has changed in the century since his last visit.

This feel of Soho as the place of youthful rebellion and cultural change appears in smaller ways in Michael Armstrong's *The Haunted House of Horror* (1969) with its young protagonists working on Carnaby Street, and Peter Walker's sadomasochistic *House of Whipcord* (1974), which begins with a gallery exhibition in Soho where young Anne-Marie realises her boyfriend has exploited personal, intimate photographs for his art.

The enduring image of 1960s Soho today is a source of nostalgia, idealising the cultural changes and freedom of the era while ignoring the danger and violence faced by many of the people who actually lived and worked in Soho at the time. This troubled nostalgia is the driving force of Edgar Wright's haunting *Last Night in Soho* (2021), where a young fashion student is transported to the glamourous sixties-era Soho in her sleep. As Eloise experiences the real 1960s Soho through the eyes of aspiring singer Sandie, she quickly realises how threatening and even deadly Soho can be. The film was shot largely in and around Soho and Fitzrovia, with key scenes of the film taking place in Soho's Toucan Pub on Carlisle Street and an imagined 1960s club called the Rialto, the exterior of which is filmed on Greek Street.

Holborn Police Station, Lamb's Conduit Street

Transport: Holborn
Underground Station
(.3 miles)

Perhaps not a true horror hotspot, but Holborn Police Station was used to film my favourite non-horror moment in a horror movie. In Gary Sherman's 1972 underground horror *Death Line* (from which this very book derives its title), middle-aged Inspector Calhoun (played by a delightfully grumpy Donald Pleasence) clashes with college student Alex, who's trying to file a missing person's report on his girlfriend, Patricia. Calhoun does not take Patricia's absence seriously and instead accuses Alex of being a thief and a troublemaker. When Alex insists that he's telling the truth, Calhoun sarcastically tells him to 'hurry back to your school Mr Campbell, there might be a protest march for you to join'. Alex's silent smirk in response shows the tension between the older and younger generations in Britain in the seventies. As Alex leaves Calhoun calls after him, 'Get your hair cut!'.

In the end, Calhoun's prejudice and mistrust of the younger generation means he fails at his work. Taking the better-late-than-never approach, he identifies the real murderer only after Alex has already saved Patricia from the cannibal living on the London Underground, who has in turn crawled back to his cave to die. While *Death Line* doesn't let anyone off easily, asking challenging questions about human morality and the class struggle in Britain, it presents the older generation as prejudiced and out of touch. The clash between students and the police in the nearby London School of Economics (LSE) and University College London (UCL) in 1968-9 would have made this message especially poignant.

Death Line was not the only film to pick up on this tension. In *Night After Night After Night* (1969) the police wrongly arrest cocky loner Pete Laver because an older officer has a grudge against the young man. In the end, the police begrudgingly release him from prison but their mutual animosity is further fuelled by the encounter. The police mistrust of youth is also referenced in *Scream* and *Scream Again and The Sorcerers*, but in both films the prejudice turns out, rather ghoulishly, to be right.

The New Dark House:
Holland Park
and Notting Hill

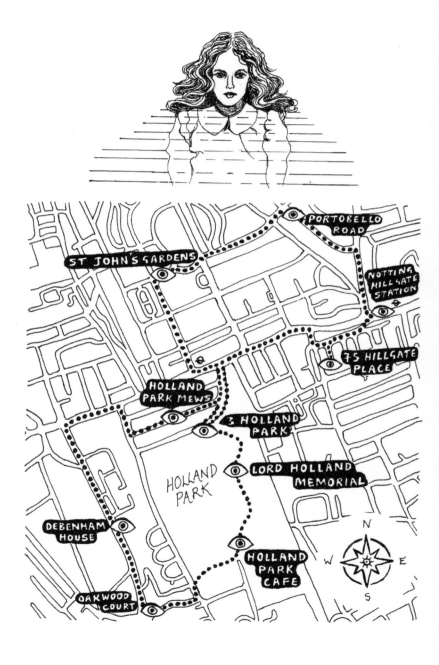

Walk Length: 3.5 miles
Starting Point: Notting Hill
Gate Station
Transport: Notting Hill
Gate Station

End Point: Notting Hill
Gate Station
Transport: Notting Hill
Gate Station

For better or worse, Richard Curtis' 1999 cloyingly romantic comedy *Notting Hill* has shaped the cinematic image of the area. On screen this is a neighbourhood of generously proportioned houses filled with floppy-haired, charming white people, private parks and cute bookshops. In reality however, this image is (at best) a localised, fantasised, aspect of a very diverse neighbourhood, but it is one that clings in the popular imagination. Horror films crack the façade of the area's quaint beauty to expose the sinister forces lurking beneath. In many cases, the fear at the heart of this area's tales of terror is grounded in deeply human concerns: turbulent relationships between mother and daughter, grief, jealousy, and painful memories. But these familiar challenges are driven by unreal, or even unearthly forces. From ghosts to demons, Martians to vampires, weird presences overwhelm the area's inhabitants, making the enticing beauty of this location dangerously misleading.

Route

✦ *Starting point: Notting Hill Gate Station. The area can be somewhat crowded, so you may find it helpful to locate a quiet space inside the station, or at the street corners outside exits 3 or 4.*

Notting Hill Gate Station is the nearest Tube station to the fictional 'Hobbs' End Station' of the 1967 sci-fi horror film *Quatermass and the Pit*. At Hobbs' End, expansion of the underground rail network reveals an unusual object that Professor Bernard Quatermass suspects may be from another world. The area was selected for the film in part because of the Notting Hill race riots of 1958, which inspired Nigel Kneale's script for the original television version of *Quatermass and the Pit*. At the climax of the film, Londoners are overtaken by an alien power lurking in their DNA which causes them to attack other citizens who do not share their 'pure' extra-terrestrial genetics. The scenes of violence, and the reason for them, revive the memory of the racially motivated riots. The director, Roy Ward Baker, had previously directed *Flame in the Streets* (1961), an allegorical film responding to the Notting Hill riots, which may have helped him to create these vivid scenes of fear and chaos.

Underlying the struggle in *Quatermass and the Pit* is the battle between good and evil present within all of us. In the next stop, this endless struggle is embodied in two famous Gothic personas.

✦ *Walk West along Notting Hill Gate, after 40 yards you will come to Farmer Street. Turn Left onto Farmer Street and take the next right onto Uxbridge Street. Then take your third left (after about 150 yards) onto Farm Place. When Farm Place curves onto Hillgate Place, look to your right to find a narrow three-storey apartment lifted above a gate between two neighbouring houses. This is 75 Hillgate Place.*

Welcome to the home of hipster vampire Johnny Alucard in Alan Gibson's *Dracula A.D. 1972* (1972). When not working for Dracula in Chelsea (see the Chelsea walk), Alucard lives just beyond the archway created by the unusual layout of these houses. The flat – painted a cheery yellow at the time of writing – is a death-trap where Alucard seduces and kills some of his female victims. Later, the tables are turned when Van Helsing corners Alucard here in his own home.

The fight between Van Helsing and Alucard is the most intense of the film, and the most unusual. By 1972, Hammer Films' Gothic villains were struggling to compete with more psychological, contemporary horror films. Pitting the 59-year-old Peter Cushing – reprising his decade-old role of Van Helsing – against twentysomething Christopher Neame as Alucard could easily be the symbolic struggle for Hammer's audience. We might expect the younger superbeing would have the edge, but Van Helsing – the Hammer hero – holds his own against the switchblade-carrying youth, at one point breaking a pool cue over Alucard's back. The fight makes it clear that Hammer is on the side of tradition when it comes to horror, and in this fight it manufactured a victory it ultimately couldn't achieve at the box office. Still, when Van Helsing finally manages to kill Alucard by running him under a shower (the one and only time this method appears in vampire lore), it is oddly anticlimactic. This domestic death has a neat resonance with our next film, which revives another Gothic tradition: the old, dark house.

✦ *Retrace your steps along Farm Place to Uxbridge Street. At Uxbridge Street turn left and take the next right on Campden Hill Road. When Campden Hill Road meets Notting Hill Gate turn left onto Notting Hill Gate, and continue for 175 yards. Turn left onto Holland Park Avenue (before Holland Park Station). After 170 yards, Holland Park Avenue curves to become Holland Park. 3 Holland Park is on your left just past the Greek embassy.*

In this impressive columned house the grieving Julia hopes to start a new life in Richard Loncraine's *Full Circle* (1977; known in the US as *The Haunting of Julia*), which will be a central film for the next few stops. After the accidental death of her daughter, Julia throws her old life and marriage away, hoping for a fresh start by moving to this new home. But the house has a tragic history of its own, and odd occurrences lead Julia to host a séance in her living room. In the darkened, candle-lit room, the medium, Mrs Flood, becomes overwhelmed and hysterical. Panic spreads throughout Julia's collected friends and as one guest goes for water, Mrs Flood whispers a warning to Julia that she must leave the house. Before Julia can ask why, there's a scream as her guest tumbles down the stairs. Despite the signs of danger, Julia ignores the warning. As she becomes entangled with its resident ghost, a young girl around the age of her daughter, this airy building becomes a haunted house. In the final scene set in her shadowy living room, Julia throws open her arms to the spirit of the young girl, who kills Julia with her haunting embrace. The home that Julia thought was her future ultimately becomes her coffin.

✦ *Retrace your steps along Holland Park. Just beyond the Greek Embassy is an entryway into Holland Park on your right. Go through the archway onto the main park path. Follow this about 140 yards and turn right onto the second path on the right; there is a small signpost indicating the Lord Holland Memorial along this path. Follow the path until it opens up onto the Lord Holland Memorial and a small pond.*

In *Full Circle* Julia visits Holland Park regularly. Here, shot just over Lord Holland's left shoulder, we see her and her sister-in-law, Lily, separate after a difficult lunch where Julia glibly insists she is over the death of her daughter, Katie. After their goodbyes Julia continues her walk, where she discovers a school at the edge of the park. As she watches young girls leave the school building, her eye falls on a blonde girl in the background whom she immediately mistakes for Katie. In a blink, the girl is gone, but the brief glimpse unsettles Julia. This is one of the first signs of Julia's haunting, and perhaps the most bittersweet because she only just insisted to Lily that she is no longer in mourning, a conversation we revisit in the next stop.

On the way, you will pass by another horror film location. As you approach the Holland Park Café, you can see on the left the Safestay Hostel. This was formerly a nurses' hostel which also played the Theatre Girls' Hostel in Norman J. Warren's *Terror* (1978). After being hypnotised at the launch party for her brother's film, aspiring Actress Ann Garrick returns to her room here with blood on her hands. With no idea what has happened, Ann begins to suspect this is the work of an old family curse. Her cousin's film retells the story of the witch that once cursed her witch-hunter family, the film itself appearing to have awakened supernatural forces which plague Ann and her cousin, James, for the rest of the movie.

✦ *If you are sitting on the bench, take the first path to your left, leading south-east away from the Lord Holland Memorial. The path stops in front of a building after 175 yards, at which point turn right and follow the path along the building until your next left. After a further 82 feet turn left again and come to the back entrance of Holland Park Café. You are welcome to call in at the café for a cup of tea, as they did in Full Circle.*

As mentioned in the last stop, after moving to her new home, Julia agrees to meet her concerned sister-in-law Lily for tea here at Holland Park Café. Their conversation is fraught: Julia has not spoken to her husband since moving out, and Lily chastises Julia for her behaviour, insisting that things will improve as she deals with her mourning. Julia gets increasingly upset and nearly shrieks at her sister-in-law that she is happy in her new life. Of course, we know from the previous stop that Julia is more bereaved than she seems.

As the film progresses, she continues to see the apparition of a young girl in the park, although Julia begins to realise it is not her daughter. One chilling encounter occurs just on the other side of the Orangery building at Holland Park Playground. On a sunny afternoon Julia decides to come to the park to photograph the children; a decision that suggests how desperately she misses her daughter. Amid the other playing children, she recognises a blonde girl from the local school, now playing in the sandpit. The girl disappears, but Julia runs over to the sandpit, where she finds a sharp file and a dead squirrel. As though in a trance she picks them up, covering her hands in blood and scaring the other children. A protective mother threatens to call the police and Julia runs home to wash the blood from her hands. The experience is so unsettling that Julia decides to hold the séance recounted on the first stop on this walk. A different kind of unhappy home is the subject of our next stop, and another troubling mother-daughter relationship.

✦ *Follow the large paved road to the left of the café, which will take you past a gated children's play area on the right. Continue 350 feet until you pass through the brick gates of the park, onto Ilchester Place. Turn right on Ilchester Place and continue until the next junction with Abbotsbury Road (around 170 yards). Once you cross Abbotsbury Road, Ilchester Place becomes Oakwood Court. Continue on Oakwood Court towards the large brick building at the end of the road. After about 500 feet, Oakwood Court curves to join another road, also called Oakwood Court – you may notice a small post box on the corner. Turn Left here to continue on Oakwood Court. After about 350 feet, before you reach the large intersection with Addison Road, you will notice on your right the entrance for 64 to 83 Oakwood Court. If you continue to the corner of this building toward Addison Road, you will notice the building juts out to make a hexagonal tower approximately where the black gate ends and the hedge begins. At the top floor of this unique structure is the apartment of the next stop. To get a better view – and the one in the film – go to the lamppost near the corner and look up to the fourth floor windows.*

At the start of Jack Gold's 1978 psychological horror *The Medusa Touch*, a camera zooms in on the top three windows of this corner flat in Oakwood Court. It is the home of John Morlar, a disillusioned telekinetic who is not afraid to use his psychic abilities for fatal and disastrous ends. At the start of the film, we see Morlar in his chair watching a news broadcast of the Achilles 6 space mission before he is brutally bludgeoned. The next morning the police are on the scene. One of the detectives discovers a pulse and rushes the unconscious Morlar to a hospital.

The story of Morlar and the attempt on his life is told through a series of visits to his psychiatrist, Dr Zonfeld. Morlar reveals to her that he has been using his psychic powers to cause deadly accidents since he was a child. From the adolescent destruction of his school and the murder of his parents to the more recent heart attack of a judge, Morlar confesses to a series of telekinetic murders that have all been reported as accidents.

The most recent tragedy, he explains, began in this seemingly ordinary flat, when Morlar came home one night to a humiliating confrontation with his wife, Patricia, and her lover, Edward. After they left, the adulterous pair were killed in a car accident, which Morlar admits he caused. Despite these stories, Zonfeld is sceptical, suggesting Morlar suffers from a combination of narcissism and guilt. To prove his abilities, Morlar crashes a Boeing plane into a tower block in central London (see the Bloomsbury walk). Zonfeld again deflects the disaster, pushing Morlar to select his next target: an upcoming American space mission... which brings us back to the start of the film.

As Morlar forces astronauts to lose communication with Earth, Zonfeld races down Oakwood Avenue – following the route you just took – and slips through the door for flats 63 to 84, which you walked past. She quickly makes her way to the top floor and knocks at his closed door. Morlar invites her in, calm and focused, as the space mission deteriorates before their eyes. In his state of callous calm, he even offers the harried psychiatrist a drink. Terrified, Zonfeld desperately tries to stop the disaster, but soon discovers that Morlar is not an easy man to kill. And, even unconscious, remains a dangerous adversary.

✦ *Turn right on Addison Road and follow for approximately 350 yards. Debenham House is on your right with blue detailing around the upper storey windows, and an elaborate brick archway labelled number 8.*

Debenham House was designed in 1905 for department store owner Ernest Ridley Debenham. As the rich blue exterior details suggest, it was known as the 'Peacock House' because of the vibrant Arts & Crafts detailing inside and out. You can experience the remarkable architecture and colours in the 1968 horror film *Secret Ceremony*, directed by Joseph Losey. In the film the rich but deeply troubled Cenci lures in down-at-heel prostitute, Leonora, to take the place of her deceased mother and form a surreal, and occasionally perverse, family. With the unwelcome arrival of Albert, Cenci's father, her past returns to haunt them both. Debenham House becomes a mirror for the alluring but disturbed Cenci: lavish and strangely attractive but held captive by its past. The extravagant, dramatic interior has also appeared on television in dramas and Agatha Christie adaptations, but *Secret Ceremony* captures how eerily dominating such a characterful house can be.

✦ *Continue along Addison Road for 175 yards until the road*
forks. Take the right fork (which continues straight) onto
Holland Park Gardens for another 175 yards. At the large
junction turn right onto Holland Park Avenue, and take
the next right, just past the Turkmenistan Embassy, onto
Holland Park. After 130 yards take the second left onto
Holland Park Mews. Stop anywhere along the mews,
though it may be easiest to stay out of traffic on either
end of this short road.

Moving from one unhappy home to another, Robert
Hartford-Davis' 1968 serial-killer horror *Corruption*
begins with a party here at number 50 Holland Park
Mews. Amid the preening models and photographers,
one model, Lynn, has brought her partner, the (much
older) prominent plastic surgeon Sir John Rowan. Lynn's
flirtatious nature and the attentions of a lecherous
photographer send the already uncomfortable Rowan
into a jealous rage. He lunges for the photographer,
knocking a light into Lynn's face and horrifically scarring
her. This accident destroys Lynn's confidence and career,
driving a guilty Rowan to remove the facial tissue and
glands of female corpses, and then living victims, to
restore Lynn's beauty.

The interior shots of the scene were filmed on set,
but we see Rowan and Lynn drive up to the wild party
here on the mews, with people standing on the balcony
and music filling the tiny lane. Holland Park Mews was
not selected for its buildings but rather its exclusive
reputation. The bourgeois-bohemian neighbourhood

lets the audience know that Lynn's circle get by as much on inherited importance as genuine talent. Lynn's sense of entitlement and Rowan's wealth push them beyond the bounds of the law and drive the gruesome acts of the film, an indictment of the class privilege and insecurity at the heart of this exclusive community.

✦ *If you haven't already, continue to the end of Holland Park Mews and turn left just beyond the archway onto Holland Park. Follow for 160 yards until it intersects with Holland Park Avenue, where you turn left. Take the next right, after 85 yards, across the road onto Lansdowne Road. This is the road just before Holland Park Station. Continue on Lansdowne Road for 350 yards and take a right onto St John's Gardens and stop at the corner.*

This innocuous street appears as 'St John's Hill' in Graham Baker's 1981 satanic horror *Omen III: The Final Conflict.* When two young mothers turn onto this road with their prams, the gentle slope behind you turns lethal, as one pram breaks free and careers into oncoming traffic, colliding with a taxi. This is no accident; the pram was under the supernatural power of Damien, the antichrist, who has come to London with the intention of killing every male child in order to prevent the second coming of Christ. Like many of the horror movies shot in the Holland Park area, this scene reveals that even the quaintest suburban neighbourhoods offer little protection against tragedy. The ease with which Damien can reach into the domestic lives of these two women is as terrifying as his rise in the ranks of civil authority, if not more so: at least we've come to expect demons in government.

✦ *Continue northeast on St John's Gardens and follow it to the right around the church for 338 feet. Cross over Ladbroke Grove onto Kensington Park Gardens, roughly straight ahead, and continue for about 170 yards. At the intersection with Kensington Park Road, cross over the road and continue straight along what is now Chepstow Villas. At the next intersection, look left up Portobello Road.*

Aggie's antiques shop on Portobello Road is a key set piece for the serial murders in Arthur Crabtree's *Horrors of the Black Museum* (1959). Here, writer Edmond Bancroft stops in to buy a dagger for his secret collection of tools used by real criminals. Noticing that some of Bancroft's purchases have been used as murder weapons, the owner, Aggie, decides to blackmail Bancroft rather than reveal his suspected murders to the police. Bancroft is initially impressed and seems to give in to the demand for money, only to turn on Aggie and stab her in the neck with a pair of ice tongs. The antique shop scenes were filmed on set, but an establishing shot of Portobello Road sets the scene. Though the stores have changed, the road today is the same collection of vivid and diverse shopfronts shown in the film.

The antiques shops of the area are also referenced in *Secret Ceremony*, the film from the Debenham House stop. Cenci's quirky aunts own an antique shop about a mile from here on St Stephen's Mews in Westbourne

Green, as they are unable to afford a space on Portobello Road. In an effort to avoid bankruptcy, they sneak into Cenci's home and take valuable objects to sell in their store. As we saw in *Horrors of The Black Museum*, the antiques stores are linked to illegal activity, but in both films there is also a sense that these objects might be haunted in much the same way that people are: Cenci's past haunts the sisters and the objects they steal, while Bancroft only seeks out objects with murder in their past. Our next stop returns us to a different, but no less dangerous past that continues to influence the present.

✦ *Continue down Portobello Road for 350 yards until it meets Pembridge Road. Turn right onto Pembridge Road and take the first left onto Notting Hill Gate, where you will see the station entrance in front of you.*

Returning again to Notting Hill Station, we revisit the fictional neighbourhood of Hobbs' End in *Quatermass and the Pit*. For centuries Hobbs' End was haunted by unusual noises and energies, once associated with the devil.[2] Professor Quatermass discovers that source of these hauntings is the buried Martian spacecraft mentioned at the start of this walk. During a press conference, an electrician drops a power cable inside the ship accidentally awakening the alien force within. The Martian energy then

2   Taking this line of thinking, critic Greil Marcus argued for the presence of the alien at the end of the film as an explanation for the occurrence of 20th century nihilism.

erupts into the city causing nearby buildings to collapse and violence to spread throughout the capital.

Quatermass and his compatriots defeat the Martian menace in the film, but off screen there is still a ghostly presence near Notting Hill Gate Station. Looking across the street and slightly west we can see the Coronet Theatre, which is said to be haunted by the ghost of a young cashier caught stealing from the till. Ashamed, she leapt to her death from one of the upper windows, where some people say they have heard her ghost walking. Though the ghost prefers to remain invisible, she is known to move things around the theatre. In *Quatermass and the Pit* the ghostly presences of Hobbs End were caused by an ancient power buried deep beneath the nearby Tube station. Just something to consider if you are leaving here on the Tube.

Looking for More?

Whether it's Cenci's troubled past, the ghost in Julia's new home, or the lingering Martian presence of Hobbs' End, many of the horror locations in Holland Park and Notting Hill are subjects of haunting. This isn't unusual for ghost-ridden London; as one of the most haunted cities in the world, films were bound to take an interest in its resident ghosts and other ways in which the city feels haunted by its past. In horror cinema, three particular hotspots are notorious for their hauntings, either literally by ghosts or metaphorically by the weight of past terrors:

10 Rillington Place (presently 8-10 Bartle Road)

Transport: Ladbroke Grove Underground (.3 miles)

Latimer Road Underground (.4 miles)

If you aren't familiar with the gruesome crimes of John Christie, you may be surprised to find that Rillington Place no longer exists. The road was renamed Runton Close in 1954 and changed again to Bartle Road in the seventies – when the original building was destroyed – to shake off its gruesome past. Such drastic action was needed because Christie, an apparently innocuous and quiet man, had murdered at least eight people and buried them in his home between 1943 and 1953. The bodies were found in the walls and garden of number 10 when Christie moved and the new owners began redecorating. Today, a square of grass between number 8 and number 10 Bartle Road, ensures that no one has to live on the old site of number 10 Rillington Place.

Before the building was destroyed and the area rebuilt, Christie's home was used for the 1971 horror film *10 Rillington Place*, directed by Richard Fleischer. This is not the only horror film to do such a thing – Stuart Rosenberg's *Amityville Horror* (1979) famously filmed exterior shots at the notorious Amityville house in Long Island – but I believe it is the only British horror film based on a true story that was filmed in the actual location. To add to the sinister aura of the film, the credits of *10 Rillington Place* emphasise that the film was shot almost entirely on location and that the building was later knocked down.

The movie centres on one particular victim, the young, pregnant Beryl who lives with her husband, Timothy, in the flat above John Christie. At the time, this area was deeply impoverished and when Beryl realises she is pregnant and can't afford the child, Christie offers to assist her in an abortion. The offer is merely as a ruse to get Beryl into his apartment and administer knock out gas before he kills her and cuts her into pieces. The reimagining is chilling, preying on the vulnerability of a poor and desperate women. In life, as in the film, Christie successfully framed Timothy for her murder, who was wrongly convicted and hanged in 1950. Christie went undiscovered until he moved out, and the bones of his victims were uncovered during a structural remodel. Timothy was posthumously cleared of murder and Christie convicted, but the presence of his victims never seemed to leave the place.

Though no one on set commented on any ghosts or mishaps while filming on location, the owner before the house was destroyed insisted it was cursed – noting failings in electricity, plumbing and a string of personal bad luck. As you can see, even today, the council is unwilling to build on the plot of land that once belonged to Christie and his victims.

Enfield: A Mini-Walk

Transport: Enfield Town
Rail Station

Enfield has a strong filmic history. It is known for Mike Leigh's *Meantime* (1983) and *Life is Sweet* (1990) – which used extras from the local community – and Alexander Mackendrick's 1951 sci-fi comedy *The Man in the White Suit*. In horror film, Enfield was first referenced as the leafy suburb where archaeologist John Banning lives in Terence Fisher's *The Mummy* (1959) (though it was actually filmed around Bray studios). It was also home to famous Golden Age horror actor William Henry Pratt, better known as Boris Karloff. As a young boy, Karloff made his first stage performance at St Mary Magdalene's Church in the Christmas play of 1896. His role as the Demon King in *Cinderella* foreshadowed his famous roles in horror films, from Frankenstein's monster to Dr Jekyll and Mr Hyde. After becoming a star for Universal Studios, Karloff would make several London-based horror films including Mark Robson's *Bedlam* (1946), Charles Lamont's *Abbott and Costello Meet Dr Jekyll and Mr Hyde* (1953), Robert Day's *Corridors of Blood* (1958), and Michael Reeves' *The Sorcerers* (1967), which are dotted through these walks.

But since then, Enfield rose to horror fame thanks to the real-life story of the Enfield Poltergeist. Between 1977 and 1979 various paranormal investigators visited two young girls in the north London suburb who were reportedly plagued by a violent poltergeist. This infamous haunting of Margaret and Janet Hodgson (and their terrified family) has inspired television shows, radio programmes, and films following both the haunting and the visits by curious investigators. Among those drawn to the case were demonologists Ed and Lorraine Warren whose visit inspired the 2016 film *The Conjuring 2: The Enfield Case*, directed by James Wan. Reimagining the story of the Enfield Poltergeist by focusing on Ed and Lorraine Warren's investigation and their relationship with the Hodgsons, the film follows the Hodgson children as they attend school at Enfield Upper Grammar School, whose Lower Grammar School Boris Karloff attended as a child. The school is not the site of any hauntings, but the film shows how distant the girls are from their peers, and in real life and on film the poltergeist activity became so disruptive that the children had to miss school.

On screen, the family lived nearby with their supernatural tormentor, at number 33 Graeme Road, though the actual location of the haunting is some 2 miles away at 284 Green Street. Confined to the home, on-screen poltergeist activity ranged from objects flying across the room and lights failing, to the youngest daughter, Janet – aged only 11 – levitating and speaking in a gruff male voice. Though the scenes of haunting are terrifying, the house is the site of a great deal of family love in the film. The domesticity is especially touching for Lorraine Warren, who has no children of her own. She is so moved by the sight of single-mother Peggy trying to hold her family together with limited resources that Lorraine and Ed use some of their wealth to bring Christmas to the impoverished family. In reality, the Hodgsons' poverty was used against them by press and sceptics: they presented Peggy as a neglectful parent whose children were so desperate for attention – or for money – that they created the illusion of a ghostly presence.

The Enfield poltergeist may be the most famous haunting in the area, but it is not the only one. Ghosts have been seen at the Rose and Crown Pub on Clay Hill, along the major carriageways through Enfield, and at Forty Hall, where visitors have reported ghost sightings since it opened to the public in 1952. The most haunted room, the Raintons' Bedroom, was known for bedclothes being disturbed as though the bed had been slept in. A group of paranormal investigators visited in 2013 and claimed to have felt a presence on the first-floor landing. Perhaps because of its reputation, Forty Hall was host to the 2010 horror short film *Short Lease*, directed by Prano Bailey-Bond and Jennifer Eiss, in which a structural surveyor finds a man dead in the foyer and is seemingly haunted as she waits for police. It is still open to the public if you fancy doing a bit of ghost hunting yourself!

Fleet Street

While this street's connection with contemporary journalism dwindles, Fleet Street has never lost its fame as the home of the bloodthirsty barber Sweeney Todd. Todd, originally a character from a penny dreadful, gained a life of his own with his fictional barber shop at 152 Fleet Street. Todd's serial murders and their resulting cannibalistic pies have been reimagined as plays and films for decades, most recently in Tim Burton's 2007 film adaptation of Stephen Sondheim's musical *Sweeney Todd: The Demon Barber of Fleet Street*.

Todd still lingers on Fleet Street in the names of one or two barber shops and his haunting presence is central to the 1936 black and white *Sweeney Todd: The Demon Barber of Fleet Street*, directed by George King. In the film, the story of Todd is told by a contemporary barber to one of his customers as he prepares for a shave. Todd's legend takes up most of the film, but in the last moments we return to the customer who is now utterly terrified to find himself in a barber's chair. He bursts out of the shop, shaving cream still on his chin, and sprints up the street towards Ludgate Hill. The power of Todd's presence is similarly enduring in horror, having inspired six plays, five horror films and myriad references over the past century.

The other haunting presence of the area is the Fleet Street Phantom. Legend has it that on Halloween in

1684 cab driver Tom Cox picked up a man, dressed all in black, for a short ride up to St Bride's Church. As soon as the man in black entered the carriage Tom's horses began to panic and refused to go up to the church gate which was the customer's destination. When the carriage door opened at the end of the ride, Tom turned to say goodnight and was confronted by a large, black bear with glowing red eyes. The bear lunged at Tom before disappearing in a burst of flame. Tom blacked out and awoke, inexplicably, in his home. The story remains a mystery.

The legend of the Fleet Street Phantom may not share the same notoriety as Sweeney Todd, but his name was revived in 1987 in the form of an educational computer game. The 'Fleet Street Phantom' literacy game, published by Sherston Software in collaboration with *The Daily News*, had children play the role of a journalist to investigate a phantom trying to sabotage the newspaper. It has little connection to Tom's tale, but it revived the haunting of Fleet Street for a generation through the 1980s.

Rocking the Cradle:
Westminster

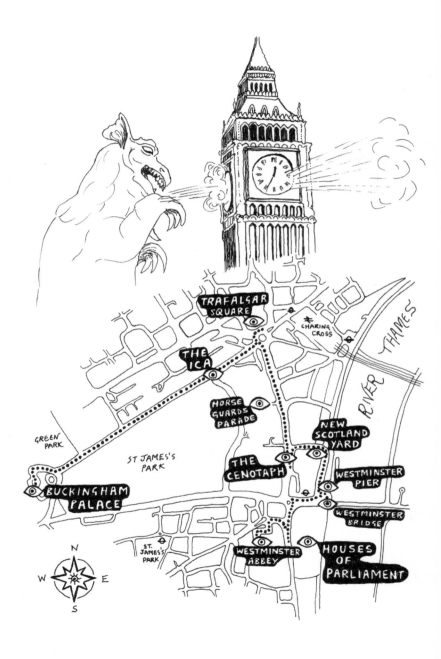

Walk Length: 2.0 miles
Starting Point:
Buckingham Palace
Transport: Green Park,
Victoria and St James' Park

Station are around 0.5 miles
from the Palace.
End Point: Parliament Square
Transport: Westminster Station

Westminster, home to Buckingham Palace, Westminster Abbey, and the Houses of Parliament, is the seat of power in Britain. Here, protesters march, royal traditions are played out and laws are decided. At one time, this relatively small area formed the epicentre of the largest Empire in the world. Since 1066 kings and queens of England have been crowned at Westminster Abbey, and parliament has met on the site of the Palace of Westminster since the 13th century. These buildings are also global landmarks: depicted on everything from book covers and t-shirts to artworks by Claude Monet, J.M.W. Turner, and street artist Banksy.

Horror cinema has taken this longstanding tradition of security and rule at Westminster and turned it inside out. Decades of horror show these buildings as the fragile core of an endangered city: some portray them attacked by monsters, aliens, and even the UK's own army, while other films present an eerily abandoned Westminster long after the government failed to protect its people. This walk will take you through the heart of British power and the films that found terror in how much trust we have to place in it.

Route

✦ *Starting Point: Buckingham Palace. The view of the Palace from the gates or from the Victoria Memorial Fountain both appear in horror films, and either make for a good photograph.*

Buckingham Palace is a London landmark, so filmmakers place it briefly in dozens of films to help establish the action in London. This includes horror films like *What Have You Done To Solange?* (1972) – an Italian giallo in which flashes of Buckingham Palace from car windows remind the viewer they are in London – or *Vampira* (1974) – in which Dracula turns into a bat in front of the Queen Victoria fountain.

When horror films feature Buckingham Palace within the plot, however, they are usually making a pointed statement about the establishment's failure to protect its citizens. Some horror films go so far as to show the government actively harming Londoners. In Bob Clark's terrifying 1979 Sherlock Holmes/Jack the Ripper crossover film *Murder By Decree*, Holmes passes by Buckingham Palace on his way to a secret meeting in Parliament Square. As his carriage passes the Victoria Fountain, we see Holmes shoot a withering glare at the palace. At this point, Holmes has discovered that the Royal family is ultimately responsible for the Ripper murders. Though he will never be allowed to hold Queen Victoria accountable, this scene reveals Holmes' disgust at the royal abuse of power.

In the 2001 *From Hell*, based on Alan Moore and Eddie Campbell's monumental comic serial of corruption, conspiracy and Masonic murder, we move inside the darkly opulent drawing rooms of Buckingham Palace for a scene between Queen Victoria and her personal physician, Dr William Gull. Gull advises the Queen on the health of her grandson, suggesting there is hope for his recovery from a sexually transmitted disease that he received from an impoverished woman, Ann Crook, in the East End. The Queen then thanks Gull, pointedly remarking on his greater service 'to his country'. The scene implies that the Queen – however obscurely – approves of Gull's murder spree as Jack the Ripper in response to his relationship with the aforementioned Ann, which resulted in an illegitimate child and thus compromising the integrity of the crown. Her approval is short-lived, however, as Gull is ultimately lobotomised due to the excessive brutality of these murders. In both films, the Queen is at the centre of the Ripper stories, abusing her power and actually seeking the death of her own subjects. Her removed sanctioning of the murders is sinister compared with the overt grisliness of the Ripper's killing, but the disregard for human life in both cases begs the question: is one truly worse than the other?

✦ *If you are facing the palace, continue to the right around the Victoria Memorial fountain, and take the first cross walk. Turn immediately left to leave the circus on the Mall. Buckingham Palace should now be directly behind you. After half a mile, the ICA is signposted on the left, after the lighted crosswalk. Stop by the stairs to the left of the ICA entrance.*

At the stairs next to the ICA entrance, bike messenger Jim picks up a pile of money in an otherwise deserted London in the 2001 post-apocalyptic horror *28 Days Later*, directed by Danny Boyle. Jim has just awoken from a coma to discover the city empty of people. As he walks through London he discovers uncanny indications of an unknown disaster – an overturned bus or discarded pile of money. At this point, Jim doesn't realise how irreparably the world has changed and his instinct is to take the money; but soon he will realise it is worthless in a world where the 'Rage Virus' has killed millions and turned the survivors into manic cannibals. Above Jim, at the top of the ICA steps, is the Duke of York Column erected in memory of Frederick William, one time Duke of York and reckless second son of George III. Frederick William famously died impoverished after lavishly spending his entire life, so there is a touch of humour to the scene when Jim finds a pile of money at the famous debtor's feet.

The scene is doubly surreal because of how quiet the Mall is. If you see the Mall in the background of other horror films, like *Murder By Decree* (1979), *Children of Men* (2006) or *The Medusa Touch* (1978), you can see how difficult it is to get this road empty, even when it is used for filming. Director Danny Boyle had to shoot this sequence in the early hours of a July morning in order to capture the road without people or traffic. As you move up the Mall to the next stop at Trafalgar Square imagine how eerily different this road would be without any cars or crowds of tourists.

+ *Continue north east along the Mall, passing under Admiralty Arch. Ahead of you is a roundabout with a statue of Charles the Second. Behind it and slightly to the left is Trafalgar Square. Cross over the roundabout at the posted crosswalks to reach the Square.*

Most people will have seen an image of Trafalgar Square before ever visiting it themselves. The square has been reproduced in postcards, photographs, and paintings – including an abstract rendering by modern artist Piet Mondrian – and has even been recreated in video games and Lego. It's a tourist spot famed for Nelson's giant column, the National Gallery, outdoor events, and the empty fourth plinth, which has hosted year-long projects by a new artist every year since 1998. As a landmark it has appeared regularly on television and film since William Carr Crofts first experimented with the camera to create a one-minute film of the square in 1890.

Trafalgar Square made its first horror cinema appearance in Universal's 1931 *Dracula* in the form of a stock shot. After Dracula's boat arrives in Whitby, the film cuts to a foggy shot of a lion statue at the base of Nelson's Column. The addition of 'London' in Gothic type overlaid on the scene helps situate the viewer. The camera then cuts to a woman selling flowers in the square before Dracula attacks her. Her death in the open air of the square demonstrates how bold and devious Dracula can be in killing his victims. It also marks the beginning of a recurring theme in the movies shot here: the dangerous anonymity of the crowd. In such a bustling location the woman disappears without catching anyone's attention, a forgotten number amid the pulsing masses of London.

Thirty years later a larger monster made its way to Trafalgar square in the form of a Godzilla-like lizard in Eugène Lourié's *Gorgo* (1961), which you may recall from the Chelsea walk. Early in the film, a fisherman captures an unusually large reptile and sells it to a travelling circus who name it Gorgo. As an advertising ploy, the circus drives Gorgo through London, passing through Trafalgar Square. Unfortunately for London, Gorgo is only a baby and his colossal mother is looking for her child. Following Gorgo's scent, she heads straight for the crowded square. Terrified onlookers flee, some taking shelter just beneath the square at Charing Cross Underground Station. As the monster stalks above, chunks of ceiling fall onto the screaming crowd below, who are no safer than those fleeing above ground. When the film was released in the early sixties, this underground scene would have evoked troubling memories of World War II, throughout which Underground stations were regularly used as public bomb shelters. At the sound of an air raid siren, people would rush to certain stations for safety, packing hundreds onto the narrow platforms anxiously waiting to hear the bombs go off overhead. These disturbing scenes were notably captured by the artist Henry Moore, whose 'Shelter Sketchbooks' – produced between 1940 and 1942 – were to provide valuable documentation of the custom, and may even be requested for viewing at the nearby British Museum.

Perhaps the most famous horror film scene set in Trafalgar Square is from John Landis' *An American Werewolf in London* (1981). When tourist David realises that he is a werewolf who murdered several people the night before, he jumps out of the cab he is sharing with his nurse girlfriend Alex. He finds himself among the tourists at Trafalgar Square and runs to the nearest police officer to confesses. Alex catches up to him and insists to the officer that David is behaving irrationally because he is grieving the death of a close friend. From that point on, David can do nothing to get himself arrested. He desperately lobs insults at the Queen, Winston Churchill, and Shakespeare, before the officer shakes him off. In this frantic state, David then tells Alex he loves her and rushes off into the crowd.

In a much quieter scene in Gordon Hessler's *Scream and Scream Again* (1970), the head of British intelligence services, Fremont, arranges a mysterious meeting in Trafalgar Square to demand an end to a project gone awry. The web of stories in the film makes Fremont's order somewhat cryptic but by the end of the film we realise this conversation refers to a governmental plan that has dire effects across the globe, from unrest in an unnamed fascist country to a series of vampire-like murders in Soho. Fremont uses the bustling square to conceal himself, as no one would suspect a secret meeting of such importance to take place in a busy tourist spot.

Thinking about all the horror scenes in Trafalgar square, the crowd is what makes this spot particularly powerful: either the masses threatened by a monster, or the secrets and dangers invisibly slipping through the crowd. This contrasts with our next stop, which is made unnerving by its arresting emptiness.

✦ *If you are facing Nelson's Column with the National Gallery Behind you, the road straight across from you (on the other side of the statue of Charles I on his horse) is Whitehall. Use the crosswalks to get to Whitehall and take it south for about 530 feet. To your right will be the Household Cavalry Museum and the entry to the Horse Guards Parade. Pass through the gates to enter the Parade.*

Every year the Horse Guards Parade fills with the pageantry and colour of military personnel for Trooping The Colour, an official military celebration of the sovereign's birthday. As the historical headquarters of the British Army, the parade celebrates the precision, gallantry, and discipline of those who don the regal red uniform. Even on normal days when tourists come to photograph the parade, there is a sense of majesty to the place, which is completely undone when we witness it following the disastrous events in *28 Days Later*.

Returning to Jim's lonely walk through London, he crosses the vacant Horse Guards Parade after roaming the empty Mall. As a single figure in this vast open space, he appears inconsolably alone. The startling 8-minute search through desolate London in *28 Days Later* was inspired by a similar journey in the 1962 horror film *Day of the Triffids*, which itself was inspired by the 1950 science-fiction thriller *Seven Days to Noon* in which the threat of a nuclear bomb leads to the evacuation of London. In *Seven Days to Noon*, when Ann – the daughter of the professor who stole the nuclear warhead – leaves the nearby military operations room, an overhead shot shows her car move through the abandoned Parade. The starkness of the scene is echoed by Jim half a century later. In both films the Parade's emptiness is hollow and uncanny, and the blanket of sand emphasises that London is as empty as a desert.

With the recent lockdowns in response to Covid-19, many of us have seen photographs of, or experienced directly, the eeriness that Jim must have felt in *28 Days Later*. The emptiness in the film however is hopelessly permanent, a situation reflected by our next stop.

✦ *Return to Whitehall through the Parade entrance and turn left, continuing south. Just after Downing Street you will see the Cenotaph in the middle of the road.*

The cenotaph – or empty tomb – has been used across the world to memorialise people whose bodies, for whatever reason, are elsewhere. World War I's trench warfare and mass graves resulted in cenotaphs across Europe to commemorate unrepatriated dead, including this cenotaph to those lost by the British and Commonwealth, built by the famed architect Sir Edwin Lutyens. Since it was first built in 1919 – and replaced in 1920 – the cenotaph's symbolic meaning has expanded to include the lost dead of various British conflicts and is now the centrepiece of the British government's Remembrance Sunday wreath laying.

The memorial is another stop on Jim's lonely walk in *28 Days Later*. The Cenotaph takes on particular resonance in this film as London has also become an empty tomb. In *The Medusa Touch*, police sergeant Duff, who is investigating a series of inexplicable deaths across London, drives past the monument and remarks: 'to build a cenotaph is to choose a million victims'. His words foreshadow the deaths of hundreds more citizens when malicious psychic, John Morlar, continues to kill after falling into a coma. In both films, the emptiness of the tomb emphasises the overwhelming number of dead in both films, which make the living seem almost insignificant.

✦ *Retrace your steps to the entrance to Downing Street and use the pedestrian crossing to cross Whitehall. Continue straight on the pedestrian road running alongside the statue of Field Marshal Montgomery. At the junction with Victoria Embankment turn right. New Scotland Yard is to your right, with its distinctive revolving sign.*

Scotland Yard has investigated murders in horror films since the 1927 silent *London After Midnight*, directed by Tod Browning. A simple establishing shot of the façade was enough to know that the police were on the case. For many films this shot would be of Old Scotland Yard, named for its former location at 4 Whitehall Place which

featured a back entrance on Great Scotland Yard. Old
Scotland Yard was a central feature of *Horrors of the Black
Museum* (also on the Chelsea and Notting Hill walks),
inspired by the Yard's eponymous collection of weapons
and evidence from famous cases. In the film, murder
weapons designed to copy those in the Black Museum
are used in a series of murders throughout west London.
The Black Museum of Scotland Yard is also visited by
actress Kitty in John Brahm's *The Lodger* (1944) at the
request of a besotted detective working the Ripper case.

While for many films the sight of Scotland Yard is
intended to be reassuring, this was not the case in Val
Guest's *Quatermass 2* (1957), which follows scientist
Bernard Quatermass as he investigates extra-terrestrial
activity at a factory in the rural town of Winnerden
Flats. After discovering an alien entity at the factory is
brainwashing people, Quatermass seeks help from the
Metropolitan Police. But when he sits down with the
police chief, he discovers a mark on the officer's hand
proving that he, along with the rest of the police force,
has fallen victim to the alien. With London fallen,
Quatermass returns to Winnerden Flats in the hope of
saving the world.

In the 1960s the face of Scotland Yard changed when
police headquarters moved to 10 Broadway under the
title 'New Scotland Yard'. This building is where police
sergeant Nicholas Angel is given the news of his transfer
out of London at the start of Edgar Wright's 2007 horror
comedy *Hot Fuzz*. Angel is moved to the sleepy town
of Sandford, Gloucestershire, because his high arrest

record is giving other officers a bad name. Angel is upset initially but becomes intrigued when a series of accidental deaths in Sandford look suspiciously like murder. New Scotland Yard is also a central location for Massimo Dallamano's giallo horror *What Have You Done to Solange?* (1972), in which Inspector Barth investigates the brutal murder of several schoolgirls. In one tense scene, Barth questions lead suspect and Italian teacher Enrico Rosseni, who grows shifty and uncomfortable as Barth asks about the most recent victim, Elizabeth, with whom the teacher had an affair. During the scene, the audience knows Rosseni is innocent, but his evasive answers reek of guilt. Unlike many other horror films, however, the inspector ultimately realises Rosseni is innocent and asks for the teacher's assistance in finding the true killer.

In 2013 New Scotland Yard moved here to Victoria Embankment and continues to appear in film and television to indicate that the police are on the case. But in horror, the police are not always the good guys, as one of the upcoming films on our walk will demonstrate.

✦ *Continue along Victoria Embankment. After about 80 feet you will see Westminster Pier across the road. To reach the pier, walk up to the junction with Westminster Bridge Road, cross Victoria Embankment using the pedestrian crossing, turn left, and walk down to the pier.*

Looking across Westminster Pier to what was once City Hall (now the London Aquarium), you can see where

Alfred Hitchcock set the scandalous introduction to his 1972 horror film, *Frenzy*. After an opening shot following the Thames from Tower Bridge, the camera settles on the Embankment and a press conference on the supposed government success at cleaning up the river. The announcement is interrupted by the shocked cries of reporters: a body has appeared, floating in the water. The corpse of a woman, a tie around her neck, signals that the elusive 'necktie murderer' has struck again. Amid the chaos, a political spokesperson is quietly escorted away from the crowd. Panicked, he asks his aide if the tie around the victim's neck is from his gentleman's club. In the first four minutes of the film, we get the sense that the government is ill-equipped to keep its citizens safe, and is in fact running away from responsibility. This cheeky jab at the both the establishment and the press turns bitter as both waste time and resources chasing an innocent man. The true necktie killer is caught in the end, but by then he has committed two more murders in broad daylight.

✦ *Retrace your steps along the Embankment to Westminster Bridge. Turn left and walk out over the bridge, then stop after a hundred metres or so and look back at the Palace of Westminster.*

The view from Westminster Bridge back to the Palace at Westminster is familiar to the most casual horror fan. It makes a brief appearance in films like *The Satanic Rites of Dracula* (1973) and *The Man Without a Body* (1957), but it is perhaps best known from *28 Days Later*. After waking up in the desolate St Thomas' Hospital on the other side of the bridge, Jim looks for any signs of life around the hospital before moving onto the bridge. About halfway along he turns to look back over his shoulder, the Houses of Parliament behind him, and shouts an echoing, unanswered 'hello'.

The scene was inspired by a similar sequence in *Day of the Triffids*, a film which follows naval officer Bill Masen who wakes up after eye-surgery to a London gone blind. Before the plant-like Triffids begin to eat the now helpless masses, Bill manages to save another sighted survivor, a schoolgirl named Susan. The two of them discover an abandoned car here on Westminster Bridge and, having seen no signs of hope in London, decide to make their way to France in hope of meeting other survivors. In both films, the stark emptiness of the bridge – usually packed with tourists – suggests that there is absolutely no hope of rebuilding society.

✦ *Retrace your steps along the bridge, and keep walking along Westminster Bridge Road, past Big Ben / the Elizabeth Tower, until you reach Parliament Square. Cross into the square and find a place to stand with a good view of the Palace of Westminster and Westminster Abbey.*

On film, the Palace at Westminster – as with Buckingham Palace or Westminster Bridge – symbolises government, power and more broadly, London as heart of the nation.

So when horror films put invading forces in and around the building, their monsters are threatening all of London and the country beyond. In *Quatermass 2*, before his visit to New Scotland Yard, Professor Bernard Quatermass seeks the help of an MP in Parliament to investigate a suspicious factory in Winnerden Flats, near the village of Ivinghoe in Buckinghamshire. He and the MP arrange a visit to the location, where Quatermass peels away from the official tour and discovers an extra-terrestrial being at the heart of the site. As with his visit to Scotland Yard, Quatermass returns to parliament to inform the government but is stopped short when he notices a tell-tale mark on everyone's hand. He has seen the same mark throughout the factory, a sign that the alien has brainwashed them.

In *Behemoth the Sea Monster* (1959) and *Gorgo*, director Eugène Lourié played out two similar stories in which enormous sea-monsters invade London, each with a face-off between the army and the monster just outside the Palace at Westminster. In *Behemoth* the monster is cornered and killed in the Thames with no damage done to the surrounding buildings. But in *Gorgo*, the army launches a missile at the monster and misses, dramatically destroying the clockface of the Elizabeth Tower before exploding. After obliterating one of London's most cherished buildings, it is hard to believe the army will be able to stop the monster (and, indeed, they don't).

The same year *Gorgo* was released (1961), John Lemont's *King-Kong*-inspired *Konga* also dropped a monster into Westminster, when a biologist experimenting with enlarging plants and animals accidentally releases a giant chimpanzee on the city. Much like *Gorgo*, the British Army are fighting the monster in Parliament Square at the film's climax, firing machine guns past the monster toward Elizabeth Tower. Unlike *Gorgo* however, the Elizabeth tower survives the attack and the monster does not. Konga collapses to her death. Her body then shrinks to its natural size, and we see her lying beside the body of the scientist who created her. This scene is a rare sign of competence by an otherwise incapable establishment, even if the Houses of Parliament do take a few bullets.

Forty-one years after *Konga* and *Gorgo*, Rob Bowman's fantasy-horror film *Reign of Fire* (2002) imagined the dragon take over of Parliament. During an expansion of the Underground rail network, a dragon is awakened by the mother of a young boy, Quinn, who manages to shelter himself and a small community from the growing dragon population. After decades of hiding in the countryside, Quinn returns to London to defeat the dragon. One of the first things Quinn encounters upon returning to the city is the heavily singed Palace of Westminster, now serving as a dragon's nest. The sight is an uncanny demonstration of the dragon's dominion over London, but also mockingly suggests these aren't the first scaly creatures in Parliament.

Alex Kurtzman's reboot of *The Mummy* (2017), starring Tom Cruise and Sofia Boutella, makes another spectacle of the Houses of Parliament when the titular mummy, Ahmanet, is freed from her prison below the Natural History Museum in Kensington. Ahmanet searches London for the tools to summon the god, Set, and as she walks through the streets, uses her powers to shatter the glass of London's buildings, turning them to sand. In an homage to 1999's *The Mummy* (a slightly goofier affair starring Brendan Fraser and directed by Stephen Sommers), Ahmanet combines grains of sand into a face that swallows the Houses of Parliament, signalling that the whole of London is under her control.

✦ *Wherever you are in the square, turn to look at Westminster Abbey. If you prefer, you can use the crosswalk to get a closer look.*

Though attacks on the Houses of Parliament are plentiful in horror, one of the first Westminster buildings to face invasion in a horror film was, in fact, Westminster Abbey. In 1955, Hammer Studios released a film that would make the production company a household name while heretically placing an alien inside England's most iconic church, *The Quatermass Xperiment*. Directed by Val Guest and based on a BBC television serial written by Nigel Kneale, the film begins with astronaut Victor Carroon emerging from a rocket test gone awry with a mysterious disease that proves to be extra-terrestrial in nature. Over the course of the film, Carroon metamorphoses as he encounters and consumes various plants, animals and people across London.

Once inside Westminster Abbey his appalling new form as a mutant blob is revealed.

Kneale set the climax of the story at Westminster Abbey because a resonant image of the location had recently been broadcast into British homes for the first time with the June 1953 televised coronation of Queen Elizabeth II. For many, it was both jarring and threatening to see the alien in the same sanctified space that they had seen the Queen receive her crown. Mercifully, *The Quatermass Xperiment*'s alien doesn't succeed in overtaking Britain. It is discovered by a BBC film crew making a documentary on the Abbey's interior, who quickly inform the authorities. Quatermass comes up with a plan to attach the BBC crew's electric cables to the scaffolding on which the alien is resting. By rerouting a huge amount of power to those cables, they successfully electrocute the Carroon-alien hybrid and save Britain. Just as the coronation represented a symbolic rebirth for post-war Britain, Kneale and Richard Landau (who adapted the story for the cinema) used the destruction of the alien to offer the hope of a better future to the war-weary generation. However, looking back today – and especially in the wider context of horror films – one can also interpret the invasion of the coronation space as an example of how precarious the institutions society relies on can be.

Returning to *Murder By Decree* from the start of this walk, having discovered that the royal family are implicated in the Jack the Ripper murders, Sherlock Holmes is called to Parliament Square by the Prime Minister. Holmes' carriage stops outside the Abbey and he enters a secret location nearby. At the meeting, the Prime Minster and other government officials demand Holmes keep his accusations to himself. In a riveting scene, Holmes shames the government and the royal family, but admits that he does not have adequate evidence to reveal the Ripper's royal connection to the world.

These two films reflect horror's wider ambiguity towards Westminster and the powerful figures who work here. The image of Westminster can offer hope through the diligence of the police or the guiding hand of the government, but in most films of the genre the government falls short. The true horror of these films does not come from the monsters that attack, but in how dramatically the government fails to protect its people, through structural inequalities that leave certain people more vulnerable than others. As you look around the square, bear in mind how precarious these notions of strength and supremacy truly are.

Looking for More?

Westminster is heavily associated with power, but there are many kinds of power in London and in its horror films. Power, both personal and political, seems to pool malevolently in certain spots across the capital, three of which make for spine-tingling horror hotspots.

The Old US Embassy, Grosvenor Square

Transport: Bond Street
Underground Station
(.3 miles)

One side of Grosvenor Square was once taken up by the US Embassy. Today the Embassy is in Battersea and the old building is being converted into a hotel, but in the 1976 film *The Omen*, directed by Richard Donner, the Embassy featured as the workplace of ambassador Robert Thorn. After moving to London to work at the Embassy, Thorn and his family experience a series of unsettling events, including strange behaviour from their son, Damien. At Damien's fifth birthday party his nurse hangs herself from the top floor of the house, quixotically declaring that she is making the sacrifice for the child. One of the photographers at the party, Keith Jennings, later tries to interview Thorn as he arrives at the Embassy. Trying to get past the press, Thorn bumps into Jennings, destroying his camera. Thorn apologises and offers to replace it, but when they next meet, Jennings discovers his camera can predict the deaths of people around Damien.

Later, in his office, Thorn is visited by Father Brennan, an Italian priest who insists to Thorn that Damien is the Antichrist. Brennan reveals that Thorn's real son was killed shortly after birth and Damien was offered as a replacement to ensure the antichrist could reach a position of global power. Thorn, thinking Brennan is trying to blackmail him, calls in security to eject the priest. Brennan continues to pursue Thorn, and you can see the results of their final exchange at the All Saint's Church hotspot on pg. 155. Remarkably, the production crew were allowed to film inside the Embassy, and Thorn's office in this scene was indeed a real embassy office, temporarily vacant at the time of filming.

The US Embassy also appears in Graham Baker's *Omen III: The Final Conflict* (1981) in which Damien returns to the UK, though this time the crew were not allowed to film inside. Instead, stock footage of the Embassy is used to show the Ambassador entering in a trance before he kills himself, leaving his job vacant for Damien to fill. Later, Damien is seen working in the Embassy, though his office is a set. There was some filming for *Omen III* on location in Grosvenor Square, where a priest sits on a bench waiting for Damien to come out of the Embassy. This priest is part of a group who have acquired sacred daggers which can be used to kill the Devil's offspring. The priest is waiting in the square to assassinate the antichrist, not realising that Damien is keeping an eye on him from the Embassy window. When Damien does finally leave in the middle of the night, he lures the unwitting priest to his death.

Most people may recognise the old US Embassy from *The Omen*, but it had actually made its horror film debut a decade earlier in Anton Leader's *Children of the Damned* (1964). In this film, scientists discover a handful of children across the globe with unique psychic abilities and abnormal intelligence. They are brought to their respective embassies in London for experimentation, but when the children become suspicious of the government's intentions, they escape. As they leave their individual embassies to regroup, six of them meet in Grosvenor Square, where the US Embassy can clearly be seen behind them. Using their telepathy, they walk off together in silence, away from the heart of the city and on to a rundown church, which you can visit on the Thames walk.

Harley Street

Transport: Regent's Park Underground Station (.1 mile from top of Harley Street)

Bond Street Underground Station (.3 miles from bottom of Harley Street)

It is hard to miss the rows of doctors' offices which line Harley Street. Since the Victorian era some of the best-known doctors in London have practiced here, while Sir Arthur Conan Doyle worked for a period in nearby Upper Wimpole Street. The connection between Harley Street and doctors is centuries old, and its reputation carries a chill of Gothic villainy. Dr Jekyll practiced on Harley Street in the 1990 Broadway play *Dr Jekyll and Mr Hyde*, and in the original book Jekyll visits the home of Dr Lanyon on Cavendish Square, at the south end of Harley Street. Victor Frankenstein establishes a practice on Harley Street in the final scenes of Terence Fisher's *Revenge of Frankenstein* (1958), allowing him to continue his dubious work under the guise of a doctor to the wealthy. Harley Street is also Frankenstein's work address in Freddie Francis' *Son of Dracula* (1974), where the half-human son of Dracula, Count Downe, comes to inquire about an experimental procedure to turn him fully human. Count Downe is set to inherit the throne of darkness from his father but, being half-human, feels a deep urge to step out of his vampiric life. Frankenstein informs Downe that he has discovered a way to make Downe both human and immortal, convincing Downe there is no downside to giving up the throne. But all is not as marvellous as it seems: after Downe leaves, Frankenstein reveals to his assistant that he plans to cause an accident in Downe's surgery, making him human only in order to kill him.

Moving away from famous Gothic villains, in Robert Day's *Corridors of Blood* (1958) the illustrious Dr Bolton has his main practice on Harley Street where he performs unusual experiments with anaesthesia. As he becomes addicted to the anaesthetic, he wanders the streets out of the respectable neighbourhood and on to the squalor of an East End pub. There he is blackmailed into helping dubious graverobber Resurrection Joe. The contrast between his elegant Harley Street home and the squalor of the pub shows, quite crudely, how far Bolton has fallen in the film.

In *The Man Without A Body* (1957), directed by W. Lee Wilder and Charles Saunders, the doctors of Harley Street use their expertise to bring the head of Nostradamus back to life. The doctor's office is suitably creepy in the film, with organs and a disembodied eye all hooked up to a machine allowing them to work independently. Yet, these doctors are not 'mad scientists' like Frankenstein or Jekyll. Their experiments in transplantation are aimed to keep people alive, and they are offering to help their patient – a millionaire named Karl with a terminal brain tumour – through a brain transplant. When the doctors test the revived head, Merritt and his assistant Jean realize that Karl has robbed the grave of Nostradamus. Once awakened, Nostradamus is resistant to joining with Karl's consciousness, as is one of the doctors, Lew, who is dating Karl's mistress. After a confrontation, Karl shoots Lew, severing his cranial nerve. To save their colleague, Merritt and Jean transplant Nostradamus's brain into Lew's body, but when he awakens he has turned into a mute monster. He then knocks over Jean, escaping down Harley Street with Dr. Merritt in pursuit. The scene is one in a long history of horror films that question the ethics of scientific advancement going back to *Frankenstein*. But, given that this film came out four years after the first successful human organ transplant, *The Man Without a Body* was likely also responding to very real fears surrounding the ethics of bodily transplantation.

Horror films have always drawn out the eerie, uncanny and terrifying potential of medicine, and over the past century there have been a plethora of doctors in horror films across the world. But some of the first cinematic maniacal medicine men worked on Harley Street, and the doctor villains of today – from Mads Mikkelsen's charming yet chilling Hannibal Lecter in NBC's eponymous TV show (2013-15) to Dieter Laser's crazed surgeon in *The Human Centipede* (2009) – owe something to the Hippocratic lineage suggested by this undeniably charged location.

Royal Albert Hall

Transport: South Kensington
Underground Station
(.6 miles)

Royal Albert Hall Bus Stop
RC (.1 miles)

The Royal Albert Hall's remarkable architecture makes it easy to identify in horror films. In Alan Gibson's *The Satanic Rites of Dracula* (1973), Doctor Van Helsing of literary fame is called to help investigate a series of occult murders in London. He decides to confront Professor Keeley, an old colleague who appears to be involved, and walks past the Royal Albert Hall on his way to the Professor's office on Elvaston Mews. There, Van Helsing discovers that Keeley is helping to develop an incurable plague for a mysterious businessman, though the title of the movie gives away who this secretive super villain might be!

In Jack Cardiff's *The Mutations* (1974), the Royal Albert Hall makes another brief appearance as characters journey from one place to another. Professor Nolter leaves neighbouring Imperial College and climbs the steps of the Hall while discussing a student who has mysteriously gone missing. As it transpires, Nolter knows more than he reveals on this walk. In both films, the professors working near the hall are able to hide the malignant purpose of their work in part because they work in this prominent area. Although not a great deal of action occurs in either film on the Albert Hall steps, here you can literally stand in the footsteps of British horror legends like Peter Cushing (Van Helsing) and Donald Pleasence (Prof. Nolter).

In the 1971 Italian giallo *A Lizard in a Woman's Skin* directed by Lucio Fulci, the Royal Albert Hall takes on the role of the Old Bailey where lawyer Frank Hammond defends his cases. Frank's wife Carol – the daughter of a prominent politician – is having unusual dreams that predict the murder of her neighbour and her step-daughter. The Hall is not the scene of intense action, but Fulci chose the distinctive building to replace the real Old Bailey because the Victorian architecture bolstered the mood of Victorian sexual repression central to the film.

If horror generally underused the Royal Albert Hall, famed horror director Alfred Hitchcock certainly recognised its potential, using the space for the climaxes of the 1934 and 1956 versions of *The Man Who Knew Too Much*. In the 1957 version, Ben and his wife search through the Hall's boxes and balconies attempting to scupper an assassination attempt on the prime minister. In the 1934 version, the lead is Bob and it is his wife Jill who leads this search. In both however, the high arches of the hall and its dramatic architecture enhance the tension of the scene, while the music playing in the concert below causes the heart to race.

Though this is a concert hall, not a strictly political space, it's interesting to reflect on the political aspects of *A Lizard in a Woman's Skin* and *The Man Who Knew Too*

Much, and the themes of the power's abuse in *The Satanic Rites of Dracula* and *The Mutations*. Perhaps the wealth of Kensington and the historic and royal connections of the Albert Hall offer a space that exudes power without taking any particular political stance, the monumental architecture of the Hall itself concentrating an uneasy and ambiguous atmosphere of foreboding.

Myth Made Manifest:
Bloomsbury

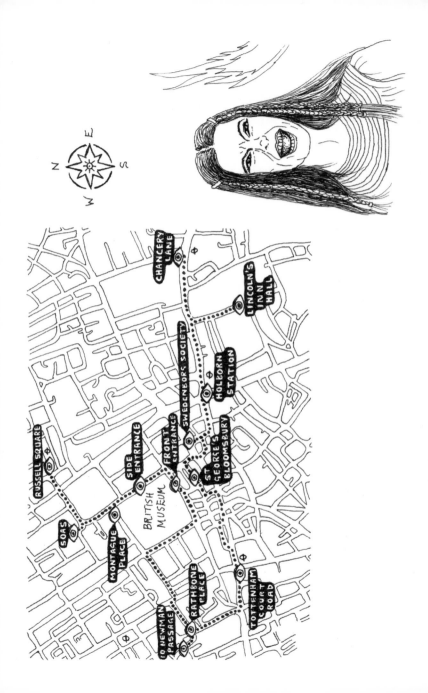

Walk Length: 2.6 miles
Starting Point:
Russell Square Station
Transport:
Russell Square Station

End Point:
Chancery Lane Station
Transport:
Chancery Lane Station

Welcome to Bloomsbury, an area humming with centuries of occult connections and significances. The neighbourhood houses some of the most mythic buildings in London, including a church by architect Nicholas Hawksmoor and the British Museum, as well as societies which practice spiritualism and alternative forms of Christianity. Horror films have made the most of Bloomsbury's longstanding relationship with the mystic and the otherworldly, bringing Egyptian gods, Druidic runes, werewolves and long-dead spirits to its streets alongside serial killers and cannibals. The terrors of Bloomsbury on screen are all the more chilling for being inspired by the area's irregular history, making even the most far-fetched storyline feel eerily possible.

Route

✦ *Starting Point: Russell Square Tube Station. You can stop outside the station, or across the street to get a better view of the Grade II listed façade.*

After failing to find what he desires in the nearby sex shops, James Manfred (whose OBE is mentioned more in this film than his first name) slips into Russell Square Station and solicits a woman on the northbound platform. When she turns him down he becomes aggressive, grabbing for her before she kicks him and takes the money in his hand. She jumps onto the departing train, leaving Manfred vulnerable to an unseen attacker. This is the opening of the remarkable 1972 horror *Death Line*, directed by Gary Sherman.

Given Manfred's behaviour, it is hard to feel entirely bad when we see him slumped on the stairs in the next scene awaiting discovery by students Patricia and Alex. Patricia immediately decides they should go for help, but when they return with the station master Manfred's body is gone. We learn later that Manfred is one of several people to disappear on the platforms of Russell Square Station, each ultimately becoming dinner for a family of cannibals – credited only as 'Man' and 'Woman' – living in the nearby tunnels. Man and Woman are the descendants of Victorian station workers, trapped when the tunnels collapsed at the nearby disused British Museum Station. The workers survived for generations on muddy rainwater and cannibalism, using this station and nearby Holborn as their hunting grounds. *Death Line*'s blurring of good and evil will come up throughout this walk, as will a number of dramatic and shocking deaths.

✦ *Turn left out of the station and continue west along*
Bernard Street, following the north side of the square.
At the corner of the square, turn right onto Thornhaugh
Street. Just head of you on the left, you will see a building
with the brass letters 'SOAS'.

The School of Oriental & African Studies – better known as SOAS – is one of several universities in Bloomsbury. Though it is not known for ghosts, many appear in its modern library in the 2021 psychological horror *Last Night in Soho*, directed by Edgar Wright. A young fashion student, Eloise, is having visions of an aspiring singer, Sandie, who lived in the same bedsit sixty years before, during the swinging 1960s. Eloise has mostly been having these visions as dreams in the night, but after she has a shocking glimpse of Sandie's death she begins to see Sandie appear in her waking life. Shaken and terrified, Eloise goes to the police who struggle to follow up on her vision of a murder, especially as Sandie's last name remains unknown, as does the surname of the man who murdered her, Jack. In the hopes of finding a missing persons report on Sandie, Eloise comes to SOAS library and searches through old newspapers documented on microfiche. As she does, the lights in the library flicker and she is set upon by a gang of faceless male ghosts, which she has also seen in her nightmares. She is terrified and tries to flee, but the ghosts appear to have her surrounded.

Cornered behind one of the stacks, Eloise decides to defend herself with a pair of shears from her design class. She attacks one of the ghosts only to be shocked when the ghost transforms into one of her fellow students. The student calls for security and Eloise flees, terrified of what may happen next.

Just before she leaves the library, Eloise catches sight of Sandie walking in the streets below. Uncertain if she can do anything to avenge Sandie or stop her fate, Eloise desperately chases after the vision, which, as we will see in a later stop, leads her deeper into the ominous backstreets of London.

✦ *Turn back down Thornhaugh Street toward Russell Square and continue straight for 620 feet. The road will change names to Russell Square. Take the second right onto Montague Place and find a convenient place to pause on the corner.*

The mysterious Mr Slade rents a room on Montague Place in John Brahm's *The Lodger* (1944). The elderly couple letting the room become suspicious of Slade, whose trips out in the middle of the night coincide with the murders of several young actresses. To make matters worse, Slade has interest in their actress daughter. The film was shot on a studio lot in Hollywood, California but this part of Bloomsbury, with its Georgian façades and links to London's bohemian underworld, was used as inspiration for the set, and is indicated by a street sign for 'Montague Place' at the start of the film.

As you may or may not have guessed, Slade's character was inspired by Jack the Ripper. The film is based on a 1913 novel of the same name by Marie Belloc Lowndes which itself was inspired by the Ripper murders of 1888 and was the source material for other horror films including *The Lodger: A Story of the London Fog* (1927) and *Man in the Attic* (1953) (which you can read more about on the Thames walk).

✦ *If you have walked down Montague Place, retrace your steps back to Russell Square and turn right so that you are heading south (as you were when you approached Montague Place). After about 50 feet this road turns into Montague Street, continue along it for around 100 yards until you reach a set of gates on your right – the side entrance to the British Museum.*

This discreet side entrance to the British Museum is the entryway used by archaeologist Matthew Corbeck in Mike Newell's *The Awakening* (1980). At the museum Corbeck's most precious find is being prepared for display: the mummified body and sarcophagus of the Egyptian Queen Kara. Like many films before it, *The Awakening* uses the British Museum to play out the story of an Egyptian curse. The narrative is inspired by Bram Stoker's novel *Jewel of the Seven Stars* (1903), which is also the source for the movies *Tale of the Mummy* (1998) and *Blood From the Mummy's Tomb* (1971), all of which have scenes in the British Museum.

Corbeck's life at the museum begins in relative peace, but as he becomes obsessed with Queen Kara he awakens the supernatural forces surrounding her which have the power to kill anyone in his way, culminating in his eighteen-year-old daughter, Margaret, falling into a coma. Despite these harrowing omens, Corbeck cannot resist breaking into the Museum's Egyptian Wing one night to perform a ritual he believes will resurrect Kara. As Corbeck lights torches and recites from an ancient text, he is so consumed with his task that he fails to notice his daughter, now miraculously conscious and having escaped hospital, is watching him from the shadows.

Margaret seems entranced as she stealthily, and slowly, makes her way towards her father. When she reaches Kara's sarcophagus, she looks on calmly as Corbeck finishes the ritual, barely acknowledging her. Once the final words of the ritual are spoken, the mummy collapses into dust. Corbeck is incensed, believing the ritual has failed, but when he looks up, Margaret has transformed into the ancient Egyptian Queen. For a brief moment he realises the true cost of his obsession before Kara kills him in a single move. The movie then cuts to an exterior shot of the British Museum as Kara opens the door to unleash her power over all of London. Since Kara was, for most of the film, an artefact, we can read her resurrection in the context of the Victorian fear of cursed objects relocated to Britain. Kara is its personification: an Egyptian power come to life to avenge itself on its Imperial discoverer, the museum, and soon the Western world.

In *Blood from the Mummy's Tomb,* Professor Fuchs takes the Corbeck role, though Fuchs keeps the mummified Queen Tera (the equivalent of Kara in *The Awakening*) and artefacts from her tomb in the basement of his home. Nonetheless, he takes his daughter, Margaret, to the British Museum where a colleague notices that she bears a striking resemblance to Queen Tera. *Tale of the Mummy* similarly moves the action out of the museum when the bandages which once wrapped the mummy Talos (the male equivalent of Kara or Tera) become sentient and break out of their display case, killing a museum guard.

These films, like Stoker's novel, are inspired by the very real fear of a curse on the British Museum. In the Victorian era, there was a widespread superstition that objects taken from Egypt and gifted to the British Museum were cursed. In his historical analysis of the mummy phenomenon, *The Mummy's Curse,* Roger Luckhurst argued that from the earliest days of importing Egyptian artefacts into Britain, Imperial anxiety bloomed in the form of such tales of horror associated with the procured artefacts. The notion of curses was fuelled largely by guilt, and by the popularity and rapid growth of Egyptian exhibits in the British Museum. Luckhurst notes that these rumours of cursed objects were at once dismissed and encouraged by the museum in the late-Victorian era, in part because the curse rumours encouraged visitors to come to the museum while also discouraging theft. These rumours encouraged an enduring association between the

British Museum and cursed Egyptian artefacts, finding its way into horror films.[3]

A legendary curse is also present in the 2001 comedy-horror *The Mummy Returns*, in which an Egyptian cult uses the British Museum to revive an ancient mummy. As part of the ceremony they have kidnapped archaeologist and historian Evelyn O'Connell to offer as a sacrifice. Her husband, Rick, and friend, Ardeth, break into the museum in an effort to save her while the ceremony is underway. The sacred ceremony is so powerful it also awakens the other mummies encased in the museum, who immediately attack the two men. The number of mummies seems unbelievable in comparison to the modest number collected in the real museum's galleries, with dozens lining an entire room. It makes for a terrifying scene while perhaps gently poking fun at the British Museum, suggesting it has more Egyptian artefacts than it can handle. We'll continue with more tales of horror in the museum at the next stop.

✦ *Continue along Montague Street for a further 500 feet until it meets Great Russell Street. Turn right, and after 350 feet you will reach the main gates of the British Museum. You can enter the courtyard if you like but be careful not to get in line for the security check, which now takes up most of the central courtyard.*

3   If the history of this curse is of interest, I would recommend reading Roger Luckhurst's *Mummy's Curse: The True History of a Dark Fantasy.*

The iconic portico of the British Museum is easy to recognise, though (as in *The Mummy Returns*) it is often replaced on film by University College London's front quad nearby. We have seen in the last stop how an obsessive interest in Egyptian artefacts can go awry, but there is so much more to unsettle and terrorise within these walls. For example, though not a location, in Terence Fischer's *Dracula* (1958), it is implied that Van Helsing has sought information in the British Museum to help defeat Count Dracula. In Piers Haggard's *The Fiendish Plot of Dr Fu Manchu* (1980), a mummy in the museum is a minor plot point; but the institution is also infiltrated because it contains potent magical herbs which the criminal mastermind Fu Manchu requires to concoct his elixir of eternal life.

The entrance to the British museum – in fact filmed in the UCL quad – is the centre for action in Stephen Sommers' horror-comedy *The Mummy Returns* (2001). When Rick and Ardeth go into the museum to save Evie, Rick leaves his son, Alex, to watch the car. Realising that his brother-in-law, Jonathan, is just as big a liability, he then has Alex watch both him and the car. The attempt to save Evie cuts between Rick and Ardeth in mortal danger and Jonathan and Alex waiting, bored, in the car until a gunshot surprises them. Jonathan, quick witted as always, then breaks the key off in the ignition. When Rick and Evie are chased into the forecourt, they find it empty. Rick instinctively heads for the car just as Jonathan and Alex appear from around the corner in a red double-decker bus. Rick demands to know what happened to his car, almost forgetting that he is trying to make an escape. Everyone piles in and the chase continues through the streets of London. The fantastic getaway-by-London-bus scene is recreated in two other London-based horror comedies: *Shaun of the Dead* and *Cockneys vs Zombies*.

In addition to the exhibitions as a source of horror inspiration, the British Library – once held in the rotunda of the museum's Great Court – makes an appearance as a source of vital information for a handful of classic horror films. A remodel in 1997 transformed the distinctive round reading room into an exhibition space, but you can still visit the central round room and get a reasonable sense of what it was like. This reading room features in Jacques Tourneur's *Night of the Demon*, a 1957 horror film inspired by the M.R. James ghost story 'Casting the Runes'. While travelling to the UK for a conference, American psychologist Dr John Holden investigates the mysterious death of his colleague, Professor Harrington. As he's doing research in the reading room, Holden encounters the powerful occultist Dr Julian Karswell, who some people believe used black magic to kill Harrington. While discussing a missing book from the library's collection, Karswell secretly slips Holden a cursed piece of paper among a stack of research notes, after which Karswell hands Holden his card. On Karswell's card is a warning in iridescent ink that Holden has only two weeks to live. After reading the card, Holden stands up to see Karswell leaving the library through a long, darkened entryway that seems to sway before him. Holden believes there is something wrong with his vision, but the experience is actually the effects of his first brush with Karswell's dark magic. When Holden looks back at the card, the warning has disappeared.

In Richard Loncraine's *Full Circle* (1977), grieving mother Julia goes to the British Museum library to learn about the young girl she suspects is haunting her home. Julia discovers that before her death, the girl was responsible for the fatal beating of a German child in Holland Park. Even more disturbing, Julia learns that the girl was killed by her own mother, who is now in an institution. This information compounds an earlier warning Julia received from a medium while holding a séance in her house, but despite the mounting evidence of evil, Julia continues to reach out to the ghostly child.

External shots of the museum also appear in the 2016 film *The Limehouse Golem* directed by Juan Carlos Medina, following police inspector John Kildare and his hunt for a serial killer in East London's Limehouse neighbourhood. Kildare ventures to the library on the hunt for the Golem of Jewish legend, having reasoned that he can whittle down his list of suspects by looking at a rarely examined book in the library. The book contains a hidden diary of the Golem, detailing each of the murders in the killer's handwriting. After handwriting samples eliminate three of the suspects, Kildare returns to the library to find the only surviving handwriting sample of his final suspect, the deceased John Cree. In the library, Kildare compares the handwritten manuscript for a play of Cree's with the Golem's diary and discovers they are identical. Thanks to the library's shelves, he believes he has found the killer. You might notice that the Library in the film is not round. The renovation rendered the rotunda of the British Museum too modern to suit the Victorian-era film, so the scenes in *The Limehouse Golem* were shot in Manchester's neo-Gothic John Rylands library. Still, the view of the exterior shots in the film are very clearly the British Museum.

✦ *If you've entered the courtyard, return to the museum gates and continue along Great Russell Street to the junction with Tottenham Court Road. Turn right, and walk up Tottenham Court Road to the junction with Percy Street. Turn left and continue until Percy Street forms a junction with Rathbone Street. Patkin's News is number 28 on the corner.*

Patkin's News is something of a haven for horror heroine Eloise in Edgar Wright's *Last Night in Soho* (2021). When Eloise arrives in London for fashion school, she takes a taxi from Paddington to the student accommodation at Ramsay Hall. After passing through Piccadilly Circus, the cabbie makes Eloise uncomfortable by commenting on her legs and then joking that if there are more pretty girls at Ramsay Hall then he will visit more often. Eloise tries to get out of the cab claiming she doesn't have the money, but the taxi driver lecherously suggests they can sort out payment another way. Luckily, Eloise spots this news agents on the corner and insists that she has to go to the shops as well. The driver reluctantly agrees to let her off at this corner, and we see Eloise hide nervously and watch as the taxi lingers outside. Fortunately, by the time Eloise buys herself a Coke, the taxi has driven off, ending the tense scene on a note of relief, but foreshadowing the dangers Eloise will encounter in Soho and in her dreams.

✦ *Continue on to Rathbone Street as it curves to your left. About halfway down the street you will see Newman Passage next to the Newman Arms pub. Turn left into the passage and walk up to number 10.*

Imagine you are looking through the viewfinder of an old film camera. In the crosshairs is a prostitute who walks down this narrow passageway, followed closely by the cameraman, to the door of number 10. The man with the camera is evidently her client, but she doesn't appear to realise he is recording her. Before they enter the building, the woman looks past him, along the passageway before leading the way to an upstairs room. As she makes herself comfortable, the camera bears down on her aggressively and her smile turns into a grotesque scream. You have just been picturing the pre-title sequence of 1960 psychological horror *Peeping Tom*, directed by Michael Powell. This scene was revolutionary because it was the first time a horror movie placed the audience in the murderer's perspective. Though this is a common trope in horror today, at its premiere the opening scene of *Peeping Tom* repulsed many, including critics: C.A. Lejeune of *The*

Observer told her readers 'It's a long time since a film disgusted me as much', and *Tribune* suggested Britain collectively should 'shovel [*Peeping Tom*] up and flush it swiftly down the nearest sewer.'

After the opening credits, a young man named Mark stops at Newman Passage the day after the murder. From a distance, he looks on as the police hold back a crowd filling Newman Passage. Mark takes out his camera to film the spectacle as the body is removed. Despite the light of day, the passage seems claustrophobically smaller in this scene, and witnessing the lifeless body feels almost emotionally cold; perhaps in contrast to our more intimate previous encounter.

The moment evidently made an impression on director Edgar Wright, who returns his heroine to Newman Passage at a critical moment in *Last Night in Soho*, where Eloise encounters a barrage of faceless ghosts in the SOAS library as well as a vision of Sandie. After running out of the library, Eloise chases her vision of Sandie through the streets and to Newman Passage. As she approaches the Newman Arms the patrons outside the pub transform into spectres before Eloise's eyes. Terrified, Eloise freezes in the middle of Rathbone Street and is nearly hit by a car. Undeterred, Eloise runs through the narrow passage and comes out on the other side back in the 1960s with Sandie's violent 'manager' Jack waiting for her. Though we do not linger on the fateful doorway of Newman Passage in *Last Night in Soho*, Wright has said that he was inspired by films of the 1960s like *Peeping Tom* and Roman Polanski's *Repulsion* when making the film, and the scene is very likely a nod to that morbidly resonant location.

✦ *Retrace your steps along Newman Place and on to Rathbone Street. Take the first right onto Rathbone Place, and when you reach Oxford Street turn left. Stop at the junction of Oxford Street, Tottenham Court Road, New Oxford Street and Charing Cross Road – a crossroads known as St Giles Circus.*

Here, amid his lonely walk through an empty London, bike messenger Jim hears his first noise – a car alarm – in *28 Days Later*. After five minutes of silence, the sound is jarring. If you have taken the Westminster walk, then you know that Jim comes to the circus after seeing most of central London depopulated. At this point, the car alarm feels impotent: far worse things have happened than a stolen car, and the owner is probably dead already.

Across the circus is Tottenham Court Road Station, where a werewolf roams free in John Landis' *An American Werewolf in London* (1981). The scene begins with a solitary man buying a cigarette on a North-bound Northern Line platform. He hears an unusual growl coming from the tunnels before looking quizzically into the abyss. Suddenly we cut to the perspective of his attacker and follow the man as he flees into the nest of tunnels. Every turn seems to take him further from safety, until finally the man makes it to an escalator, where he trips. The camera moves to the top of the escalator so we can see the victim, helpless, as the werewolf approaches.

In *Reign of Fire* the monster of Tottenham Court Road is a dragon, unearthed during an extension of the Tube network. The awakened dragon escapes and its offspring take over Britain. At the climax of the film, survivor Quinn must return to the former station to kill the dragon. The station is utterly unrecognisable save for a wrecked Underground carriage jutting up from the ground, which Quinn uses as shelter from the dragon's flames.

Across the street from Tottenham Court Road is Centre Point tower, an ominously iconic structure designed by architect George Marsh in the early 1960s that provides the setting for a telepathic tragedy in Jack Gold's *The Medusa Touch* (1978). In the film, psychiatrist Dr Zonfeld has been trying to convince her patient, John Morlar, that he is not telepathic. Taking up Zonfeld's challenge to prove his abilities, Morlar uses his psychokinesis to crash a Boeing 747 into the tower. Today, in a post 9-11 world, the resonance of such scenes can be too charged for general audiences. With the exception of Allen Coulter's mildly controversial *Remember Me* (2010), such plane crashes have been avoided or, in a number of films, re-edited for the sake of sensitivity, most notably Sam Raimi's New York set *Spider-Man* (2002). In *The Medusa Touch* however, the crash is only one tragedy among many leading to a dramatic climax at Minster Cathedral.

✦ *Continue along New Oxford Street and then Bloomsbury Way for 500 metres, until you reach the church of St George the Martyr, Holborn.*

This domineering church, completed in 1730, is one of six in London built by architect Nicholas Hawksmoor. Hawksmoor, who also served as Christopher Wren's assistant in the rebuilding of St Paul's Cathedral, is associated with Freemasonry, a key plot point in the 2002 Ripper-inspired film *From Hell*, directed by Albert and Allen Hughes. The film is based on an epic graphic novel of the same name by Alan Moore and Eddie Campbell originally published as a serial between 1989 and 1998. In both the film and the comic book Sir William Gull, a Mason and Royal Physician tasked with an epoch-defining act of ritual murder by Queen Victoria, believes Hawksmoor's churches to be situated around London in a magically resonant pattern. The main church in the film is Christ Church in Spitalfields (which appears on the East End walk), but in the graphic novel, Moore delves deeper into Hawksmoor's identity as a Freemason, including St George's, in a carriage tour Dr Gull dictates to his terrified assistant Netley, as they plot the murders of Ripper fame against the dark energies of a deeply occulted London. In opposition to the potentially macabre powers of the architecture, the crypt currently houses the Museum of Comedy.

✦ *Continue along Bloomsbury Way for 400 feet and you will see Swedenborg House on the right at the corner with Barter Street.*

Another building with occult associations, the Swedenborg Society of London has met in Bloomsbury since the 19th century. You can still see the distinct signage on the face of the building here on Bloomsbury Way. The Society was dedicated to the works of Emanuel Swedenborg who, in addition to being a scientist, wrote several theological treatises that are considered tantamount to mystical revelations. Swedenborg believed God appointed him to reveal the true spiritual meaning of the bible and to write a new guide for Christians to follow. His works served as the basis of a new church, and also include *The Heavenly Doctrine*, which suggests that the Last Judgement has already occurred and that Swedenborg himself witnessed the second coming. There's a great deal written about Swedenborg, but here we'll consider his mark on horror history.

Swedenborg is said to have inspired the work of renowned Irish author of ghost stories J. Sheridan Le Fanu. Swedenborg's influence is particularly visible in the short story 'Green Tea' (1872) where key aspects of the tale were based upon Swedenborg's theological tenets, while aspects of his peculiar cosmology appear in 'Madam Crowl's Ghost' (1870). Though neither story was made into a horror film, Le Fanu became an essential figure in horror cinema thanks to his short story 'Carmilla' (1872) which centred on a lonely female vampire. 'Carmilla' has been adapted for film more than a dozen times and in at least four languages between Lambert Hillyer's *Dracula's Daughter* in 1936 and Emily Harris' *Carmilla* in 2019. In Britain the most noted adaptations are probably Hammer's *The Vampire Lovers* (1970) and *Lust for a Vampire* (1971).

Swedenborg was also an influence on the artist William Blake, who annotated some of Swedenborg's later books. Blake's *The Great Red Dragon and the Woman Clothed in Sun* (1805-1810) features in the Thomas Harris horror novel, *Red Dragon*, which was originally published in 1981 and later adapted for film twice; initially as *Manhunter* in 1986, and later as *Red Dragon* in 2002. In both the 2002 film and the book, serial killer Francis Dolarhyde becomes obsessed with Blake's painting and tattoos his back to mimic the dragon of the painting. Blake's influence suffuses several of Alan Moore's graphic novels including the menacing anarchist parable *V For Vendetta* (1982-89), but it is in *From Hell* that Blake's disconcerting imagery, namely *The Ghost Of A Flea* (1819-20), is perhaps most pointedly oriented to reflect the imperial horror of the British establishment whose horrors 'gave birth to the twentieth century.'

✦ *Continue along Bloomsbury Way to the junction with Southampton Place. Turn right and walk along to the junction with High Holborn. Turn left and continue to the junction with Kingsway. Holborn Underground Station is on the other side of Kingsway.*

Returning to *Death Line* from the start of this walk, the cannibal Man also hunts for victims at Holborn Station. When Alex and Patricia get separated after going to the theatre, Patricia finds herself alone on the platform at Holborn Station where Man kidnaps her. This time, Man does not have hunger on his mind: his wife,

Woman, has died and he is searching for a new mate. Once Alex realises that Patricia has not come home, he seeks help at the nearby police station only to be met with cynicism from Donald Pleasence's Inspector Calhoun (which you can read more about at the High Holborn Police Station hotspot).

In 1935 something eerily similar happened when two girls went missing at Holborn Station, never to be seen again. Thanks to its proximity to the British Museum, the station inspired rumours that it was haunted by an Egyptian ghost whose remains were housed at the museum, likely the spirit of Amun-Ra, chief of the Egyptian deities. Since no bodies were discovered of the missing girls, people suggested that Amun-Ra may have taken them. The Egyptian theory was bolstered by strange marks supposedly carved into the tiles between British Museum Station and Holborn Station after the First World War. Though nearly two decades separated the missing girls from the carvings, the idea of Amun-Ra was so present in cultural memory, that the two phenomena became linked in popular ghost lore. Perhaps *Death Line* offers another solution to the case; after all, their bodies were never found.

✦ *Continue along High Holborn for 350 yards and turn right onto Great Turnstile. After 190 feet continue onto Newman's Row, which runs along the east side of Lincoln's Inn Fields. Mid-way down this side of the field on your left is the gated entrance to the Honourable Society of Lincoln's Inn. The red and white brickwork of the Inn's Great Hall stands out from the rest of the square.*

The Honourable Society of Lincoln's Inn is one of four Inns in the Court of London to which barristers belong. Here they are called to the Bar – qualifying them to argue in court – and come together as members of the society, which is both a social and professional space. The Great Hall, opened by Queen Victoria in 1845, acts as a dining space and events venue which people outside of the society can hire.

The Great Hall plays the role of Old Scotland Yard in *The Limehouse Golem*. The film begins with the murder of John Cree, who died in his home in New Square (which happens to be around the corner). At the Honourable Society of Lincoln's Inn, protagonist Kildare receives vital evidence linking John Cree's death to an unsolved series of murders which he calls the Golem killings. If you are able to go in the courtyard, you will recognise the establishing shot of Scotland Yard, though the offices Kildare uses inside were not filmed in London.

Looking back to the square, in *Day of the Triffids* (1962), naval officer Bill Masen walks along Lincoln's Inn Fields in search of other sighted survivors after a meteor shower renders most of the world blind. When he walks through the square, a Triffid in the garden turns its head to follow him. The Triffid does not attack, so Masen fails to notice it, but he does observe the scattering of blind people bumping into one another and feeling their way around the square. He stops to watch one blind man slowly climb the elaborate fountain you can see at the corner of the square opposite the gateway to The Great Hall.

Though not captured on film, the south side of the square is home to the Royal College of Surgeons' Hunterian Museum. The museum houses a vast array of anatomical specimens and medical instruments and models built around the collection of celebrated 18th century surgeon Sir John Hunter. Hunter is sometimes described as the father of scientific surgery, and was a likely influence for the character of Doctor Thomas Bolton in Robert Day's period horror *Corridors of Blood* (1958). Bolton is a troubled surgeon trying to improve anaesthesia for more accurate surgery, and in the opening scene does a surgical demonstration that would have been like those Hunter pioneered. The museum's collection is also a draw for those fascinated by the morbid, with its vast collection of human and non-human specimens in jars. Such pieces are often an included set-piece in horror films, whether in Frankenstein's laboratory, or in the corner of an infamous doctor's study.

✦ *Retrace your steps along Newman's Row and Great Turnstile to High Holborn. Turn right on High Holborn and continue for 350 yards. Chancery Lane Tube Station is on your left.*

Chancery Lane Tube Station appears in the 1985 spirit-vampire horror *Lifeforce*, directed by Tobe Hooper, whose previous works include *The Texas Chainsaw Massacre*, *Eaten Alive*, and *Poltergeist*. In *Lifeforce*, three seemingly human creatures in suspended animation are discovered on a vast alien ship and returned to Earth for study.

Once they wake, these space vampires break out of their containment facility and proceed to suck the living souls out of innocent Londoners. One vampire, credited rather innocently as 'Space Girl', gets to St Paul's Cathedral and begins to use the building as a beacon to drain the souls of citizens, beaming them up to a ship in orbit. Included in the shots of the ensuing chaos is Chancery Lane Tube Station. The station the film shows us was actually a set, modelled on the real station entrance. SAS officer Colonel Colin Caine fights his way through the crowd, stepping over and pushing past soulless bodies surrounding the station. Below ground the Tube tunnel is lined with piles of corpses, while above a double-decker bus explodes, presumably from the force of spirits ripping through it.

It seems appropriate to end our tour of Bloomsbury on the film *Lifeforce* because, like the area itself, it presents an impressive melting pot of horror myths and legends. The film draws the ancient legend of vampirism into unnerving proximity with the architectural immensity of London, much like the revived mummies of *The Awakening* and *Tale of the Mummy* did at the British Museum. The final scenes of *Lifeforce* are an apocalyptic vision that parallels the second coming of Christ, evoking both the transcendent accounts of Swedenborg and the visionary images of William Blake. Fusing an eclectic assortment of beliefs and powers, arcane myths and contemporary resonances, *Lifeforce* is a warped mirror of the otherworldly appeal of Bloomsbury as it continues to captivate us in horror cinema, but equally on the streets that surround us today.

Looking for More?

Bloomsbury has an association with the occult, and for good reason, but there are many other places to visit across London where horror films have brought out the occult history and myths of the city. Below are three such horror hotspots, drawing on a wide range of underground beliefs:

St Paul's Cathedral

Transport: St Paul's
Underground Station
(.1 mile)

St Paul's Cathedral is an icon of the London skyline, and (like Trafalgar Square and Big Ben) has been used by filmmakers as a signal to mark that action is taking place in the city. To take two examples, in Burr Steers' *Pride and Prejudice and Zombies* (2016), hero Fitzwilliam Darcy is depicted battling on a wall that protects London from zombie invasion with St Paul's as the only recognisable feature behind him; in Tony Scott's erotic vampire movie *The Hunger* (1983), new vampire Sarah Roberts flees New York to escape the police, but the film ends in a vast apartment overlooking St Paul's Cathedral. In both films, the iconic potency of St Paul's locates the characters in a single frame.

In films where the cathedral is more prominent, its dome is a symbol of power, either political, social or mythic. The aforementioned 2001 film *From Hell*, and the graphic novel on which it was based, highlight the Masonic history of the cathedral as a source of power. The graphic novel goes into great detail on this subject when royal physician Dr William Gull gives a tour of Masonic buildings throughout London to his coachman, Netley.

Included on the tour is St Paul's, which, according to Gull's crazed interpretation, forms the ultimate Masonic symbol of masculine power. In Gull's interpretation of Masonic lore, the cathedral is actually a temple to the Sun God, Apollo, and was intentionally built over a ruined temple to the goddess Diana. The doctor explains that Masons are concerned with eliminating female power while harnessing male power, and so the cathedral's replacement of Diana with Apollo is as much a monument to chauvinism as it is to a Masonic architectural victory over the city.

Gull goes on to tell Netley that when Christopher Wren dug into the foundations of the old cathedral after the Great Fire, he is said to have discovered the remains of a Roman Temple, believed to be the Temple of Diana. When he rebuilt St Paul's Cathedral on top of it, he was erecting a temple to a male figure (Christ) on top of a place of female worship. Though there is some historical basis for a temple in the approximate location for St Paul's, there is no evidence of it being dedicated to Diana. Still, the legend of Diana's temple is persistent enough that you can find YouTube channels and 'Hidden London' tours that capitalise on it.

Perhaps because of the lack of historical substance, the film *From Hell* does not include Gull's Masonic theories, though it is worth noting that several killings happen near locations Dr Gull discusses in the graphic novel. The film also visually ties the cathedral to the Freemasons when a Masonic initiation ritual takes place in an underground meeting near the cathedral. St Paul's also looms over the city throughout the film, filling the blood-red sky with an infernally oppressive presence.

Even if we do not accept the Masonic history of St
Paul's, its supposed construction over a Roman temple
of Diana is relevant to the climactic scenes of Tobe
Hooper's *Lifeforce* (1985). By the end of the film a female
space vampire, credited rather humorously as Space Girl,
has established herself as a transmitter within St Paul's
Cathedral, employing its vast resonant architecture to
extract the souls of Londoners by beaming them up
to her ship. When the astronaut who had originally
discovered her, Carlsen, rushes into St Paul's to stop
Space Girl we see the cathedral's pews, populated with
a few dead bodies, beyond which a beam of blue light –
indicating human souls – bursts through both the altar
and the dome to the spaceship hovering above. The
exterior shots were filmed at a model village, the star
attraction of a Dorset theme park known as Tucktonia
(permanently closed in 1986), while the interior is a set
that doesn't entirely resemble the real location. Space
Girl's choice of the crypt as the transmission point for her
channelling of Londoners' souls might be interpreted as
a charged location of female energies. In destroying the
altar and dome of St Paul's with these transmissions,
she is tarnishing the sanctity of the church in an action
that returns immense female power to the rumoured
former temple of Diana. The film does not specifically
mention Diana, or any Roman gods for that matter,
but a scientist, Dr Fallada, deduces that the vampires
have been visiting Earth for centuries, inspiring ancient
vampire myths and potentially other powerful beings.
It isn't too grand a leap then to suggest that Space Girl

could be returning to her temple. The clear parallel between Diana's role as goddess of the hunt and Space Girl's hunt for human souls would suggest as much.

Even if Space Girl did not previously visit as the goddess Diana, her return to Diana's temple harnesses an ancient female power that nearly destroys the city. In a counter to this power, Space Girl is nearly defeated by two men. Carlsen makes the first attempt to stop her, but becomes transfixed and joins her, naked, on her pseudo-altar. Shortly after, Carlsen's SAS colleague, Caine, arrives. He brings Carlsen to his senses and throws him a spear. Carlsen impales Space Girl and himself, in an act evocative of Van Helsing staking Lucy in *Dracula*. Though she has lost, Space Girl is not dead. She and Carlsen ascend to the alien ship and depart for another planet.

Lifeforce is one of two horror films notable for being set inside St Paul's. The other, Peter Sasdy's *Hands of the Ripper* (1971), sets the final scenes in the cathedral's impressive Whispering Gallery. *Hands of the Ripper* focuses on Dr John Pritchard's attempt to cure Anna – the orphaned daughter of Jack the Ripper – of her trauma-induced murderous episodes. Unfortunately, Pritchard loses control, and after Anna stabs him she goes to visit the Whispering Gallery with the doctor's blind future daughter-in-law, Laura. Laura has no idea Anna is capable of murder, and after deciding to show her the gallery's unusual acoustics, suggests that Anna move to the opposite side of the dome so that they can whisper to one another. On her way, Anna goes into one of her murderous trances, becoming catatonic. Unable to see what is happening, Laura grows concerned and as she feels her way around the edge of the gallery Anna takes her by surprise and tries to strangle her. At that moment, Pritchard and his son arrive on the scene. From below Pritchard calls up to Anna, demanding she release Laura and come to him. Eventually, Anna obeys, leaping to her death over the railing of the gallery.

The Imperial War Museum, Lambeth

Transport: Lambeth North
Underground Station
(.3 miles)

Elephant and Castle
Underground Station
(.4 miles)

As a Jewish woman who likes horror films, I think the genre tends to underrepresent Jewish occult practices and mythology. One of the few British horror films to engage with Jewish mysticism is the 1966 *It!* (also called *Curse of the Golem*), directed by Herbert J. Leder, in which a young curator, Arthur Pimm, discovers that an unusual statue belonging to a London museum is the original golem of Kaballac lore: a man of clay created by Rabbi Judah Loew ben Bezalel in 16th century Prague to act as protector of his village. The museum is intended to resemble an institution like the V&A but is in fact filmed here at the Imperial War Museum. Once Pimm discovers how to awaken the golem, he uses it as a minion to rob the museum and eventually murder his boss. Pimm finally realises the full extent of the danger when he realises he can no longer control the golem.

Outside the threatening world of *It!*, the Imperial War Museum has never had a golem in its collection, but the site has been the source of some supernatural activity.

From 1814-1930 it was the location of London's largest asylum, the Bethlem Royal Hospital, known colloquially as Bedlam. The move was incited by a scandal when some of the disturbing and horrific practices that took place in the institution were brought to light. These draconian approaches to 'caring' for the mentally ill have since made the name of Bedlam infamous and inspired Mark Robson's 1946 film *Bedlam* staring Boris Karloff. In the film, young woman Nell Bowan is forcibly admitted to Bedlam by Karloff's George Sims after she tries to reform the horrendous treatment of patients at the hospital. Though the move to Lambeth supposedly brought a fresh start to Bethlem Hospital, some of the most horrific and dangerous criminals of the time were sent to the asylum, including Edward Oxford – who tried to assassinate Queen Victoria in 1840. Either because of the notoriety of villains such as Oxford or the disturbing practices at Bethlem, the site was said to be charged with a haunting atmosphere. During WWII the building was used by the Women's Auxiliary Air Force, and many of the women lodging there became disturbed at night by strange sounds. The complaints were so persistent that the detachment had to be moved.

The Maddening Crowd:
Covent Garden
and Leicester Square

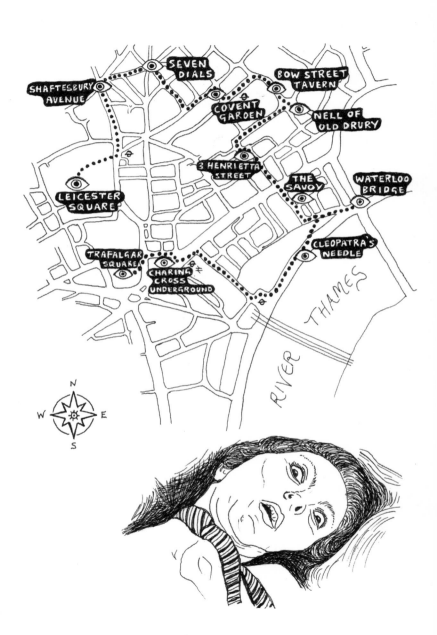

Walk Length: 2 miles
Starting Point:
Trafalgar Square
Transport: Charing Cross
Underground

End Point:
Leicester Square Station
Transport: Leicester Square
Underground

The area around Covent Garden to Leicester Square is a concentrated microcosm of London: bustling, ever-changing, and steeped in history. Over centuries it has fluctuated between wealth and poverty. While once it was known for its thriving fruit market, theatres and gin halls, thievery and disease, it is now perhaps most commonly encountered as a manicured tourist attraction. Throughout all of its iterations however, it has remained an indisputable centre of energy. In horror cinema, the crowds that flow through its busy streets and central square are as deadly as any monster. Imagine the feeling of hundreds of people frantically rushing down to an Underground station, or a panicked crowd pushing each other directly into oncoming traffic at a busy circus. The frisson of energy that ripples through this area is intoxicating, reminding us of the dangers that lurk beneath our pedestrian encounters with the modern city. But as you walk through this area, try to think also of how much the distinct character of these streets is defined by the busyness of its people, and what it might mean to find them empty. Horror films, cunningly, have built upon both the manic dread of crowdedness and the awful despair of vacancy.

Route

✦ *Starting Point: Trafalgar Square. If possible, find a spot from which you can see the discreet entrance to Charing Cross Tube Station on the south-east corner of the square.*

If you have completed the Bloomsbury walk, then you are already familiar with Trafalgar Square. Here Dracula takes his first victim in Tod Browning and Karl Freund's *Dracula* (1931), David tries to get himself arrested in John Landis' *An American Werewolf in London* (1981) and, in Gordon Hessler's *Scream and Scream Again* (1970), a secret government meeting is held. For this walk, we'll focus on the south-east corner of the square, near the statue of Henry Havelock, and the unobtrusive entrance into Charing Cross Underground Station. This small staircase is where people flee underground to escape the rampaging monster in Eugène Lourié's *Gorgo*, Britain's very own *Godzilla*. The narrow entry gives a sense of how crowded and claustrophobic the scene is, as hundreds of terrified people huddle under Trafalgar Square while the gargantuan lizard rampages above.

The darkened platforms of Charing Cross Station are where US Medical Officer Scarlet and two children, Tammy and Andy, escape in Juan Carlos Fresnadillo's *28 Weeks Later* (2007). The film begins just months after Danny Boyle's *28 Days Later* (2002), with Tammy and Andy reuniting with their father on the Isle of Dogs after the US Army has quarantined the city from an outbreak known as the Rage virus. Tammy and Andy break quarantine and bring the virus back with them when they come across their infected mother in their former North London home. As the virus spreads through the quarantined zone, the US Army panics and orders that everyone be killed. Thanks to the help of one sniper and an army medic, Scarlet and the children escape several attempts on their lives. In one such attempt, Scarlet saves them from an aerial attack by driving below ground into Charing Cross Tube Station. The feat would actually be impossible; as you can see, the entrance is far too narrow for a car, and the wider entrances around the corner (which you will see at the next stop) have fortified dividers splitting the space in half.

In the darkness of the Underground, the three of them struggle down the escalator over piles of dead bodies and become separated. Unbeknownst to them, lurking on the platform is Tammy and Andy's father, Don, who has been turned into a pseudo-zombie by the Rage disease. In the dark, Don kills Scarlet and then attacks Andy on the station platform. When Tammy arrives, she shoots their father but is unable to save Andy, who collapses, bleeding, to the floor. As Tammy leans over her wounded brother, Andy asks hopelessly if he will become like their father, a mindless entity possessed by a biochemical urge to murder. This kind of charged confrontation on the Underground is a theme we will continue to explore at our next stop.

✦ *At the south east Corner of Trafalgar Square is a pedestrian crossing that takes you onto the Strand.*

Follow the Strand to the left away from the roundabout.
After about 200 feet Charing Cross Station will be on
your right.

In Christopher Smith's 2004 film *Creep*, party-girl
Kate falls asleep on the platform of Charing Cross
Underground, and awakens to find herself trapped
beneath ground and pursued by a haunting figure
that lives off the station's platform. The entrance to
Charing Cross Underground that we witness in the film
is actually the Stratton Street entrance to Green Park
Station, around 20 minutes walk west of here. Still, the
ticket box and Underground sequences of the film were
shot in Charing Cross Station on the disused Jubilee
Line platforms, with additional sequences shot at the
now-abandoned Aldwych Station (also a horror hotspot).

Charing Cross Underground is also where Ian goes
to escape fear-eating Harvesters in Dario Piana's *The
Deaths of Ian Stone* (2007). Ian is a seemingly ordinary
man who dies in a car accident before waking up to
find himself mid-way through another life. After dying
several further times and waking up to a series of new
lives, Ian discovers he is being hunted by supernatural
beings known as Harvesters who end his current life
timeline whenever he gets too close to Jenny, a woman
who also continues to reappear in his new lives. Tired
of dying in this endlessly morbid 'Groundhog Day', Ian
convinces Jenny to hide on the Underground because
the empty train carriages make it hard for the Harvesters
to trace him. Their peace doesn't last long and once the

train arrives at Charing Cross, they spot Harvesters joining the train. As the Tube doors close, Ian and Jenny jump out onto the Jubilee Line platform along with one of the Harvesters. Desperate, Ian spots a train at the parallel platform and they make a run for it. The arrangement of Charing Cross Station makes this scene possible, and ramps up the tension as Ian and Jenny dive for the platform pursued by one of the Harvesters. Unfortunately, the train speeds off at the last moment, leaving Ian to face an awful fate.

These two films demonstrate a pattern in horror where the Underground might be perceived as both a place of sanctuary and threat, where our pursuit of safety might lead us directly into unexpected confrontations with the very terrors we wish to avoid.

✦ *Continue straight along the Strand for 148 feet, then turn right onto the pedestrianised Villiers Street. Continue along Villiers Street for 175 yards until you come to Victoria Embankment Gardens on your left. Enter the gardens through the first gate and continue straight along the brick path until you reach a large, open area. Cross over the area towards the large potted palm tree beyond. Continue straight, following the path roughly parallel to the Thames for 175 yards until you reach the statue of Robert Raikes. Turn right at the statue and follow the path to Victoria Embankment Road. At the pedestrian crossing, cross over the road to the riverside walkway, and turn right, heading for the large Egyptian statues. The obelisk in the middle is Cleopatra's Needle.*

Cleopatra's Needle is reproduced digitally for a pivotal scene in the Hughes Brothers' Jack the Ripper horror film *From Hell* (2001). In the scene, a prostitute named Polly Nichols stares up at the needle in awe while eating grapes in the back of a carriage. A man in the shadows behind her tells her that many men died bringing the obelisk to London, before he strangles her from behind, ensuring her dying vision is the Needle. The man is Jack the Ripper, and the grapes he offered her will become an essential clue in his capture.

Cleopatra's Needle is significant in *From Hell* because of its Masonic ties. If you have visited the St Paul's Cathedral hotspot, you will know that the Ripper is killing prostitutes as part of a quasi-Masonic ritual. When the Ripper takes Polly to the Needle, he imparts its mystical history, highlighting the death and tragedy that appear to charge its ominous form with a portentous dread. As with the mythical pre-history of St Paul's Cathedral – which was allegedly constructed atop a pagan temple – there is some historical truth to the Ripper's superstitions. Though gifted to Britain decades before, Cleopatra's Needle did not begin its journey to London until 1877, thanks to the financial support of Sir William James Erasmus Wilson. Wilson was a Freemason and fellow of the Royal College of Surgeons, as is the Ripper in *From Hell*. According to the cosmology of the movie (and the graphic novel by Alan Moore and Eddie Campbell upon which it is based), the obelisk is said to be inscribed with symbols resonant for Masonry, and to have been placed along an important ley line bisecting London, making it a protective talisman of sorts for the city. Some people believe that when the shipping crews died transporting the Needle to London, their sacrifice cemented the sacred power of the obelisk; a power that could be said to manifest through the demonic actions of the Ripper.

✦ *Retrace your steps along the Embankment and continue to Waterloo Bridge.*

Across the road on this side of the river is the great Georgian era Somerset House, whose clocktower is visible in the opening narration of the 2010 horror-comedy *Burke and Hare*, directed by John Landis of *American Werewolf* and the *Thriller* music video fame. The rest of the film takes place in Edinburgh, following the two famous graverobbers in their attempt to kill people and sell their bodies to doctors at the local medical university. The opening scene alludes vaguely to bodies hanging at the gallows, and the Neoclassical architecture and open courtyard of Somerset House make for a visually dramatic setting for an execution, instilling the scene with a sense of institutional history and judicial gravity. Somerset House also makes a brief appearance as a New York street in Tim Burton's horror comedy *Sleepy Hollow* (1999). Filmmakers recreated Victorian New York for the film by using locations throughout the United Kingdom, including Oxford and London. In the final scene of the film, Ichabod Crane returns to New York City, and as he and his paramour Katrina walk down the street, the building behind them can clearly be identified as Somerset House.

Turning back toward the Thames, a dead body is found on this very stretch of the Embankment in Alfred Hitchcock's 1927 silent film *The Lodger: A Story of the London Fog*. Only the latest in a series of grisly murders, the body sparks a press whirlwind that ultimately leads to an innocent man being hounded (almost to death) by panicked citizens. Originally, Hitchcock intended to include a shot of a body being pulled from the river, but it was cut from the film due to a combination of censorship and uneven lighting. The scene, if it had stayed in the film, would no doubt have been deeply shocking for the time. Over forty years later, Hitchcock would return to this area to film a different body floating up onto the Embankment in *Frenzy* (1972).

✦ *Retrace your steps along the Embankment towards Cleopatra's Needle. Take the first right onto Savoy Street, following it up to the Strand. Turn left onto the Strand and walk a further 120 yards. The entrance to the Savoy Hotel is on your left.*

The five-star Savoy Hotel has been synonymous with luxury since it opened in 1889, but it became internationally famous during World War II when it served as a meeting place for world leaders like Winston Churchill and Charles de Gaulle. This reputation made it popular with Americans and may indeed be why Dr John Holden stays at the Savoy in Jacques Tourneur's supernatural horror *Night of the Demon* (1957).

After visiting the country mansion of mystical cult leader Julian Karswell, the sceptical Holden learns that he has been cursed to die, before returning to his hotel room. As he walks through the hotel, Holden hears an eerie tune in a hallway, but cannot find its source. As he scrutinises the emptiness, the door behind him opens, making him jump. Thankfully, it's only his other colleagues, whom he invites to his room for a drink. He whistles the unusual tune for them, and one historian recognises it as an ancient Irish song about the devil. As Holden processes this, the same man notices that all the days after the 28th – Holden's predicted date of death – have been inexplicably ripped from his calendar.

The link between the supernatural and the Savoy Hotel goes beyond cinema. Notice the feline topiary beside the entrance to the Savoy: these unique cats are modelled after the Savoy's cat, Kaspar. Kaspar is not a pet, but rather a sinuously carved statue who joins tables of thirteen at the hotel to ward off bad luck. The superstition started in 1898 when a wealthy man named Woolf Joel hosted a party at the Savoy at which only thirteen people attended. The superstition of thirteen naturally came up during dinner, with someone mentioning the belief that when a table of thirteen convened, it meant bad luck for the first person to depart. To ease his guest's mind, Joel was the first to leave the table and was shot weeks later, confirming the suspicions of his guests. The Savoy quickly took action to keep its patrons safe and included a member of staff at any table of thirteen until 1927 when architect Basil Ionides carved Kaspar to act as the ceremonial fourteenth place at the table.

✦ *Continue along the Strand and take the next zebra crossing to your right across the road (about 100 feet away). This will take you to Southampton Street. Continue straight along Southampton Street for 160 yards until it curves. Follow the curve around The Ivy restaurant onto Henrietta Street. Number 3 Henrietta Street is on your left just past the restaurant.*

Returning to Hitchcock's *Frenzy*, this is the home of Bob Rusk, a fruit and vegetable merchant in the nearby Covent Garden Market. Rusk's close friend, Richard Blaney, is wrongly accused of a series of murders performed by the 'necktie murderer', and when Rusk overhears Blaney's girlfriend, Babs, argue with her landlord over Blaney, Rusk offers his apartment to her as a place to stay. He leads Babs up to his apartment on the second floor, and lets her in, commenting that Babs is 'his type of woman'. The door closes, and in silence, the camera moves backwards down the staircase and out the door where the noise of the street drowns out Babs' screams; Rusk, the real necktie murderer, has taken another victim. This scene is a classic example of Hitchcock's direction. The burgeoning silence as the camera retreats builds tension for the audience who know that Babs is trapped, and yet our knowledge remains futile as we're drawn helplessly back through the casually ignorant people in the market below.

Later in the film, when Blaney turns to Rusk for help, Rusk again offers Blaney his apartment as a hideout. Rusk insists that they leave for his home separately to be less conspicuous. Taking Blaney's bag with him, Rusk arrives at his flat first and fills the bag with Babs' clothing before calling the police. Once Blaney arrives Rusk is all smiles and leaves just before the police arrive, who unceremoniously arrest Blaney, using the bag of clothes as evidence against him. Following his prosecution and imprisonment, Blaney injures himself in order to be moved to a less secure hospital from which he's able to escape, before sneaking back here to Rusk's flat, intent on killing his former friend.

✦ *Behind you is Covent Garden Market – which we return to in a later stop. You can walk through the Market or around it to Russell Street on the right. Continue on Russell St for 130 yards, then turn right onto Catherine Street. The Nell of Old Drury Pub is on your right after 100 feet.*

Still in the world of *Frenzy*, Blaney goes to The Nell of Old Drury early in the film and overhears the necktie murders being discussed. The interior scenes were actually filmed on set, but an establishing shot shows off the pub's distinctively carved bay window. The pub has stood here since the 1700s, and it is believed that Hitchcock's father visited it when he frequented Covent Garden Market as a greengrocer. It is likely that Hitchcock remembered the pub when he came back to London to film *Frenzy*.

Thinking back to the stop prior to this, we can tell how meticulously Hitchcock had planned the drama of *Frenzy*.

As a London boy whose father had worked in the area, he was determined to have the layout of his film be as realistic as possible. The main locations for the film are all tightly packed around Covent Garden, ensuring that the characters can move through the space in real time. The close-set crowded locations also create the uneasy sense of a trap, as both the police and Rusk close in on Blaney.

✦ *Retrace your steps along Catherine Street, and take a left on Russell Street. Then, take the first right onto Bow Street. After about 100 feet, the Bow Street Tavern is on your right.*

This tavern appears in *Frenzy* under its old name, the Globe Public House, though it is easily recognised from its bright red façade. Blaney, at the start of the film, works for the Globe and lives in one of the rooms above. However, when he is caught stealing a small drink from one of the beer taps he's immediately fired, beginning a chain of events that lead to Blaney's implication in the necktie murders.

This is also the pub where Babs works. After she seemingly disappears for a day her boss calls the police to inform them that Babs left with Blaney the night before. When Babs returns to collect her things, her boss tells Babs what he's done, warning her to stay away from Blaney. This sparks an argument in front of all of the customers, after which Babs quits. When she rushes out she runs straight into Rusk, who chillingly cannot wait to offer her a place to stay.

✦ *Continue North on Bow Street for about 100 yards and turn left onto Floral Street. Take the next right onto James Street, and walk down towards Covent Garden Market. The market can be crowded so find a quiet place to stop and look at it.*

When Hitchcock returned to London after fifty years of making films the US, he was determined to recreate the market here as he remembered it: lively, loud, and colourful. Rusk works at the market, and we see him there as the charismatic, charming salesman. But he is also able to hide his misdeeds within the market, even taking advantage of its late hours to dispose of Babs' body by hiding it in a potato truck. Hitchcock captured the energy of the bustling market, and the constant noise and movement add to the frenzy of the police and newspaper attacks on Blaney. This is a place of drama and uncertainty, something our next horror film picked up on.

Covent Garden is home to the Royal Opera House, which we passed on the way to and from the Bow Street Tavern, and was the setting for Terence Fisher's adaptation of *The Phantom of the Opera* (1962). Notably, the film moved the action from Paris to London, and though filmed on location at Wimbledon Theatre, the Royal Opera House is supposedly where the enraged Phantom and his hunchbacked assistant threatened the players and kill several members of the opera company. In a key feature of the film, the passages beneath the Royal Opera House lead to the Thames

embankment. No such tunnels exist at the Royal Opera
House, but they may have been inspired by the hidden
tunnel that ran between the nearby Nell of Old Drury
pub and Theatre Royal. The pub gets its name from the
17th century actress Eleanor 'Nell' Gwyn, one of the first
ladies on the English stage and mistress to Charles II.
The tunnel running between the pub and the theatre,
where Nell occasionally performed, became part of
London lore when it was suggested that Charles II could
have used it to visit his mistress in secret. Though
there is no hard evidence, the story of hidden tunnels
in Covent Garden no doubt helped make the tunnels
in *Phantom of the Opera* seem plausible to the audience.

✦ *Retrace your steps along James Street and continue
towards Covent Garden Station. At the station, turn right
on to Long Acre. Continue on Long Acre for 120 yards and
turn right onto Mercer Street. Continue on Mercer Street
for 175 yards until you come to Seven Dials – a seven-way
road junction with an elegant multi-faced sundial.*

In Robert Day's *Corridors of Blood* (1958), eminent
physician Dr Thomas Bolton, played by Boris Karloff,
volunteers his time in a woman's hospital in Seven
Dials. The distinctive star-patterned streets of the Seven
Dials were recreated at MGM Studios in Borehamwood
to mark an area of extreme poverty at the time the film
was set (the 19th century). Here we see Bolton treat
destitute, starving sex workers and their malnourished
children, offering them both kindness and respect

as well as medical attention. The scenes show that Bolton is a good man before he goes mad during his experiments with anaesthetic. Once addicted to the drug, Bolton is blackmailed by an innkeeper, his wife, and their menacing friend, 'Resurrection Joe'. In a manner reminiscent of Burke and Hare's ghoulish activities earlier on this walk, Joe forces Bolton to write death certificates for the bodies he claims to have robbed from graves so that he can sell them legitimately to medical schools. When one of the women Bolton treated at this clinic is brought before him, he realises that Joe is up to much worse than graverobbing.

✦ *Walk down Earlham Street (between a Caffè Nero and the Lumas Art Centre at the time of writing) to the junction with Shaftesbury Avenue. Turn left on to Shaftesbury Avenue and find a quiet place to stop.*

In the seventies and eighties, Shaftesbury Avenue was part of London's red-light district, lined with pornography theatres and smut shops. This leering atmosphere is captured as characters walk through Soho in both *Death Line* and *An American Werewolf in London*, where bright lights draw male punters in for a good time. Though the character has changed somewhat, the crowded avenue is still of interest to horror fans. In *28 Weeks Later*, Tammy and Andy along with their two military protectors, walk down a deserted Shaftesbury Avenue. As they proceed through the quiet streets, dark in the twilight with the occasional flash of neon, the city feels like an uncanny wasteland. Shaftesbury Avenue also appears in the final scenes of Gerard Johnson's serial-killer horror *Tony* (2009), as the titular character walks through the bright lights of the area towards Piccadilly Circus. The congested nature of Shaftesbury Avenue effectively camouflages this serial killer amongst the crowd, making his unremarkable looks chilling in their banality: Johnson seems to be suggesting that anyone in this city could be a murderer, there could even be a Tony brushing past you right now.

✦ *Continue on Shaftesbury Avenue and take the second left after Earlham Street onto Charing Cross Road. Continue on Charing Cross Road for 175 yards before you reach Leicester Square Station. At the corner, turn right onto Cranbourn Street and after about 100 yards you will come to Leicester Square, a lively square populated by multiple cinemas.*

In Freddie Francis' light horror movie *Son of Dracula* (1974), Count Downe, the half-human half-vampire son of the Prince of Darkness, comes to Leicester Square to enjoy the lighter side of life, blending anonymously into the city's crowds. He even performs a song on the piano at a nearby Soho club, which is unsurprising given that Downe is played by renowned musician Harry Nilsson. Nilsson presents Downe as a rock vampire, attracted to the neighbourhood for its creativity and bohemian leanings. In the sixties, the Empire, visible on the north side of the square, was remodelled to include a dance hall, while the Prince Charles Cinema on Leicester Place brought a more diverse repertoire of films to the area, originally showing pornographic films before moving on to screenings of cult classics like Jim Sharman's notorious *The Rocky Horror Picture Show* (1975). At the same time, the legendary Cavern in the Town (now the Leicester Square Theatre) held gigs by The Rolling Stones, Sex Pistols, and The Who. This is exactly where Downe and his family advisor (played by Ringo Starr) would go on a night out in London, a comfortable venue for his vampire persona. As if to confirm the connection, the film momentarily shatters the fourth wall when Downe stops at the window of a music shop and sees the album cover for *Son of Dracula* – recorded by Nilsson to coincide with the release of the film.

Leicester Square, like Shaftesbury Avenue or Covent Garden, allows horror directors to play an unsettling game of hide and to seek. The surge of the crowd is a form of comfortable camouflage that may offer protection for the likes of Downe, but also conceals any manner of sin or sinner. Films like these defy the common horror trope that you are safer amongst people than you are alone, and remind city dwellers that places like London are always threatening, primarily because of the people who inhabit them.

Looking for More?

The horror films of Covent Garden and Leicester Square feed into the crowds and history of the area, but many of them also deal with madness. Either the madness of a specific person – like Tony in *Tony* or Bolton in *Corridors of Blood* – or the madness of groups and institutions – as with the terrorised masses in *Gorgo* or the overeager police in *Frenzy*. But madness may be present in any city, especially a large and crowded city like London, and there are plenty of other horror hotspots that play on this theme:

Piccadilly Circus

Transport: Piccadilly Circus
Underground Station
(0 miles)

The bright lights of Piccadilly Circus have appeared in hundreds of films since its cinematic debut in the 1896 Lumière Brothers one-minute film, *Piccadilly Circus*. And, like Leicester Square, horror directors have embraced the popular tourist spot as a site to play with the violent hysteria of the crowd.

The ultimate example of this is the famous scene in John Landis' 1981 horror-comedy *An American Werewolf in London*, in which the dense traffic of Piccadilly Circus turns a wolf escape into an orgy of death. After nearly killing himself to keep from turning into a werewolf, shaken tourist David ducks into a porno at the New Eros Theatre, just below the famous Piccadilly billboard. Once inside the cinema, he confronts the ghosts of his previous victims who demand he kill himself in order to release their souls to heaven. During the argument, night falls and David transforms into a werewolf, attacking another man and the cinema attendant. When the police investigate, they discover were-David and shut down the theatre, but – in true London fashion – their barricade draws a crowd. As the crowd starts to push against the barrier, were-David breaks free, decapitating a police officer and running off into the square.

From there the true carnage begins. The wolf confronts a bus that careens out of control, sending the circus into chaos. Cars are overturned, the crowd panics and flees in all directions, falling into the streets, rolling under cars and crashing into each other. We even see a body thrown violently through the glass of an ATM vestibule. Ironically, the entire series of death and destruction is not caused by the wolf; his only victim was the initial police officer. The dozens of dead and injured are all caused by the panic of the frenzied masses.

The scene in *An American Werewolf in London* is not only a fan favourite, but has been cited as a classic by other horror directors. Edgar Wright has mentioned this as one of his favourite films, and discussed this scene. So it is no surprise that he also uses Piccadilly Circus in his recent horror film, the 2021 *Last Night in Soho*, though the scene is shot in a more quietly eerie mood. In one of the 1960s sequences, aspiring singer Sandie and her would-be manager, Jack, drive past the Eros Fountain and Sandie expresses a cheerful confidence that she will do what it takes to be on stage in Soho, not realising what that determination will cost her.

All Saint's Church, Fulham

Transport: Putney Bridge
Underground Station
(.1 miles)

In Richard Donner's *The Omen* (1976), Robert Thorn meets with Father Brennan in nearby Bishop's Park. It is the second meeting between the dying priest and Thorn in which Brennan tries to warn Thorn that his son, Damien, is the antichrist. Thorne is still resistant to the idea, arguing with Brennan and then leaving in anger. As he goes, Brennan becomes engulfed in a sudden, supernatural thunderstorm. Recognising the thunder as a threat, a terrified Brennan flees to find sanctuary, spotting the tower of All Saint's Church. At the church gates he finds them sealed shut, and climbs over them as lightning streaks the sky. Fearing for his life, he races through the cemetery and collides with the firmly locked front door. Frantic and frustrated, Brennan then goes around to a side entrance of the church, hammering loudly to be let in. A crack of thunder and lightning catches his attention. He stands back from the door and looks up to see the lightning rod at the top of the tower crack. In a swift movement, it falls from the tower and impales him where he stands.

This astonishing scene looks so real because no digital effects were used. The film crew tied the lighting rod to a fishing line at the top of the church tower and a corresponding spot in the cemetery below. For the risky stunt, the rod was released and sped down the line hitting the ground only centimetres behind the actor, who went limp at the right moment. As we are here, feel free to recreate Brennan's race for safety; just leave the trick with the lightning rod to the professionals.

Kensington Mansions, Earl's Court

Transportation: Earl's Court
Underground Station
(150 meters)

This nineteenth-century brick mansion block is home to Carol Ledoux in the 1965 psychological horror *Repulsion*, directed by Roman Polanski. Carol is a young woman with a deep fear of the world around her, and in particular the attention she receives from men. When her sister leaves for a romantic weekend with her boyfriend, Carol's anxiety reaches a fever pitch. Soon Carol is unable to go to work and unable to eat, slowly going mad within the suffocating walls of her apartment – walls which seem to reach out with dozens of hands to molest her. By the end of the film, as an uncooked rabbit rots in one corner and a dead body in another, this merging of her frantic mind with reality is both gruesome and terrifying.

Most of the rest of the film takes place in nearby South Kensington, but Earl's Court has been visited by other horror films. In *The Dark Eyes of London* (1939), heroine Diana stays temporarily in Earl's Court while investigating the unexpected death of her father. In Peter Collinson's *Straight on Till Morning* (1972), wide-

eyed Brenda moves to Earl's Court to begin her new life
in London. On Earl's Court Road she runs into Peter, on
whom she develops a dangerous crush. Later, she steals
Peter's dog in a desperate attempt for his affection and
brings it back to her apartment on Hogarth Road. When
she goes to return the dog, Peter is revealed to be a serial
killer who murders both Brenda and his pet. The next
day, Peter casually returns to Hogarth Road and buys a
newspaper with Brenda's disappearance occupying the
headline. No one would suspect he killed her, nor that
such a twisted story could unfold in this quiet, domestic
part of west London.

Mind the Doors: The London Underground

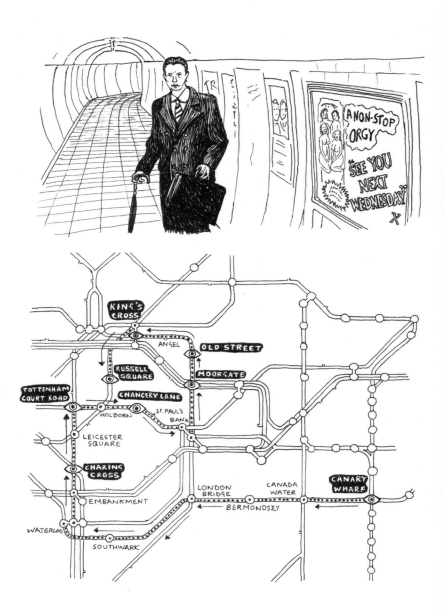

Distance: Depends on your route, but it can take an hour or more to travel the route below.
Starting Point: Canary Wharf Station

Cost: At the time of writing an adult single ticket for the route described here costs £6.
End Point: Leicester Square Station

Moving through London on its vast Underground network can change people. As we descend into the Tube, we see frequent commuters erecting invisible shields, not speaking to anyone and contorting themselves in order to hide their faces in a book, phone, or newspaper. Perfectly competent individuals can become nervous tourists on the Underground, staring at maps like jigsaw puzzles. We seem to retreat into an almost animal state, flinging ourselves at closing doors and forcing ourselves violently onto overcrowded carriages as though our lives depended on it. This fear is brought vividly to life in horror films, where primal creatures dwell in the tunnels, and lingering for too long on an empty platform could cost you your life.

The London Underground starred in its first horror film in 1967 with the fictional station of Hobbs End in Roy Ward Baker's *Quatermass and the Pit*, and has regularly resurfaced since to frighten and beguile with the thought of what lies beneath. Unearthing buried evils on the Underground is a popular theme of horror, but the stations can also provide shelter to the terrorised. Moving deep into the Underground can force confrontations with characters' innermost fears, causing them to become either more or less human. In this walk we'll venture below ground to discover if the Underground of horror is truly trap or sanctuary.

When I lead this walk for groups, we usually stop at each station platform in the order recommended below, but for those already familiar with the Tube network – or feeling adventurous – I suggest you create your own route out of the stops I've highlighted. Think of the London Underground as your playground. Start or stop at any point, try to use as many or as few lines as possible, or get off at a stop to go above ground and visit other horror hotspots or walks. Just don't miss the last train.

Route

✦ *Starting Point: Canary Wharf Underground.*

While the skyscraper lined streets above Canary Wharf Station play host to their own form of corporate horror, the station itself is best known for its role in Danny Boyle's *28 Days Later* (2002) and its sequel, *28 Weeks Later*, directed by Juan Carlos Fresnadillo in 2007. In *28 Days Later*, the Underground provides a shelter when hapless protagonist Jim, played by Cillian Murphy, takes refuge in an abandoned newsagent inside the station with the help of fellow survivors Selena and Mark. To keep out of sight from anyone infected with the volatile 'Rage' virus, Selena and Mark have been using a metal screen to hide themselves, while sustaining themselves on the preserved food they have found. The malnourished Jim is also able to eat for the first time after awakening from a coma, while Selena and Mark recount the country's collapse as a result of a viral epidemic turning many of Britain's inhabitants into zombie-like cannibals.

In a deleted scene, the three walk the tracks of the Docklands Light Railway from the station into the city, chancing upon a train carriage that had once been turned into a hospital. Putting a triage centre in a Tube car suggests that, for a brief time, the Tube lines were one of the relatively safer places to be found in London. As the characters walk through the carriage, Mark takes Jim aside to impress upon him that even in a city as dense as London, there are probably no other survivors.

His words however appear to be wasted on Jim, who finds a mobile in one of the abandoned bags on the train, and immediately tries to make a call.

In *28 Weeks Later*, the entrance to Canary Warf Station houses a candlelight memorial with photographs of some of the people lost to the infection. This film occurs long after *28 Days Later*, after all the Rage victims are believed to have died off as the result of starvation. The US Army is slowly returning people to London, using a barricaded Isle of Dogs as a quarantine zone. Children Tammy and Andy return to England after being separated from their family, arriving at Canary Warf where their father – a rare survivor in England – is waiting. As they leave the station, the family passes by the memorial on their way to their new home, a reminder of how many were lost to the virus. The great loop of the Thames around Canary Wharf and the Isle of Dogs makes this a natural refuge – but when the Rage virus returns, its limited access points leave few places to run, turning this sanctuary into a claustrophobic hellscape. The DLR tunnels are one of the few ways to escape both the infected and the army, who have decided to eliminate all survivors rather than risk another worldwide pandemic.

✦ *Take the westbound Jubilee Line five stops to Waterloo. Change for the northbound Northern Line, and go two stops to Charing Cross Station.*

If you have previously taken the Covent Garden or Westminster walks you will be familiar with Charing Cross

Underground and its roles in horror cinema. If not, then here's an inventory of instances in which this location has provided an anxious context for horror happenings. In Eugène Lourié's monster movie *Gorgo* (1961), hundreds of frightened Londoners hide in Charing Cross Station to escape the rampage of a several-hundred-foot tall lizard as it stalks the streets above. In *28 Weeks Later*, Charing Cross Underground Station also plays a sanctuary for Tammy and Andy when they are trying to escape the pursuing army. Once on the platforms, though, they encounter their Rage-infected father. This is a significant moment psychologically as well as emotionally for the children. Earlier in the film, Tammy and Andy discovered that their father, Don, left their mother for dead when it looked as though she might become infected. Rather than denying or ignoring the past by simply escaping their father, Tammy is forced to confront and kill Don. In doing so, she saves her brother, protecting him in the way Don failed to protect their mother.

In Christopher Smith's *Creep* (2004), young socialite Kate becomes trapped on the Underground when she falls asleep at Charing Cross Tube Station and misses the last train. Kate is terrorised for the rest of the night, first when a drunk colleague, Guy, attempts to assault her, and later by the human monster living just off the platform, Craig. Craig follows Kate, attacking Guy and then Mandy, a homeless woman living in the hidden backrooms of the station. When he finally captures Kate, she breaks free and comes upon 'Surgery Suite 12', a hidden bunker where it appears that clandestine surgical experiments were once performed. In the dilapidated bunker, Kate discovers a series of cots, one of which belonged to Craig. Though she doesn't realise it until later, Craig was born on the Underground, and has lived his entire life just off the Charing Cross platforms. Though it is not clear in the film why the Surgery Suite was abandoned, one can assume Craig lived most of his adult life alone as a subterranean hermit, and as a child witnessed horrific surgeries that he would later attempt to perform on his victims.

Kate, by contrast, evolves as a result of her experiences on the Underground, developing a social awareness that contrasts with her previous self-centeredness. This is marked by the final scene of the film where the once glamorous party girl collapses, covered in mud and blood, on the Charing Cross platform. Her position is now reversed from when a homeless man asked her for change and Kate refused in obvious disgust in one of the film's earlier scenes. In her now dishevelled state, a commuter mistakes Kate for a homeless person, giving her a few coins. Kate laughs, simply happy to be alive. Then, in the final moment of the film, she looks to the camera, implying that the very same thing could happen to us.

✦ *Stay on the northbound Northern Line and continue two stops to Tottenham Court Road.*

You are now on the northbound Northern Line platform, the site of an attack scene from John Landis' seminal horror comedy *An American Werewolf in London* (1981). In one of the film's most iconic scenes, we witness a train arriving on this platform here. As its commuters exit onto the platform, one man lingers to purchase some cigarettes from a vending machine. After the train departs, he hears a strange growl coming from the tunnel. Glancing at the darkened archway, he hears another low growl echoing onto the platform. He decides to run for it, the chase continuing through the tangled passages of Tottenham Court Road Station. He falls however, just at the foot of an escalator, making him easy prey for the werewolf in pursuit.

Though *An American Werewolf in London* was filmed in the station, a recent redevelopment has widened the narrow platforms and removed the distinctive tiles. This renovation project inspired a horrifying discovery in the 2002 fantasy horror *Reign of Fire*, directed by Rob Bowman. While digging to expand the platforms (a motif familiar from the development works at Hobbs End in *Quatermass and the Pit*), workers awaken a dragon dormant beneath the city. The construction crew chief, Karen, manages to escape to an elevator with her son, Quinn, but when the dragon climbs through the hole to get out, it crushes her. At the end of the film, Quinn is forced to return to the ruined station to confront the dragon, and the loss of his mother. Through flashbacks, we see Quinn face the anguish of his mother's death, and the persistent reality of his grief. Unlike the passenger in *An American Werewolf in London*, Quinn survives, gaining strength from his mother's memory to defeat the dragon. Much like Kate, his return to the Underground offers him an opportunity for transformation, and like Tammy and Andy, allows him to begin the painful work of resolving family trauma.

✦ *Change at Tottenham Court Road for the eastbound Central Line two stops to Chancery Lane.*

Chancery Lane Station appears in Tobe Hooper's sci-fi horror *Lifeforce* (1985). Here, SAS soldier Colonel Colin Caine stumbles upon a horrific scene as the souls of commuters are extracted from their bodies by a spirit-sucking space vampire. Caine is unaffected, trying to get through the screaming onlookers as they watch spirits leave their corpses behind and cascade out of the station. Unlike the other films we have encountered so far, there is no clear lesson to be learned here, or indeed any sense of safety to be found on the Underground. A quick shot of the platform shows people frantically crawling amid the piles of bodies, rendering the station a catacomb of chaos.

Step out of this station, and you will see that while *Lifeforce* depicts Chancery Lane Station with a large ground-floor entrance, it is actually only accessible by a narrow staircase. An entire establishing sequence was recorded on set and was designed to look like a newer station than this smaller Central Line stop. So why did the filmmakers choose it? Perhaps because the station is close to St Paul's Cathedral, where the apocalyptic climax of the film takes place (pg.127), or possibly because it is only a short walk from Fleet Street, a location with its own unique history of ghosts and murder. Whatever the reason, the scene is spectacular, with the blue light of souls streaking out from the Underground, as a double decker bus explodes in billows of orange flame.

+ *Continue on the eastbound Central Line two more stops to Bank. Change for the northbound Northern Line, and go one stop to Moorgate.*

In *28 Weeks Later*, infected Londoners surge down the stairs of Moorgate Tube Station while another group marches across Trafalgar Square. By accessing the tunnels, the infected ensure no place in London is safe. Their presence throughout the city also reveals the extent to which the US Army have failed to contain the virus, despite firebombing the quarantine zone.

If zombies leave you cold, keep your eyes open for the spectre of a man in blue overalls who might be seen walking the platform. The ghost of Moorgate Station has many potential origin stories, but this ghost's modern clothing suggests he may be a victim of the Moorgate rail crash. On 28 February 1975, a train on the Northern City Line failed to stop at what was then the end of the line. The train crashed into the wall, killing 43 people and injuring dozens more. Thankfully, according to witness accounts, the ghost is less malevolent than the Rage victims.

+ *Continue northbound on the Northern Line one stop to Old Street.*

The southbound platform of the Northern Line at Old Street Station is the site of a supernatural murder in Russell Mulcahy's *Tale of the Mummy* (1998). Inspired by Bram Stoker's *Jewel of the Seven Stars* (1903), the film tells the story of the cursed ancient Egyptian king, Talos, whose remains are brought to the British Museum by a group of archaeologists. As the planets align, Talos' funereal wrappings come to life, attacking various individuals throughout the city and taking a specific body part from each victim. In an effort to stop Talos from returning, one of the archaeologists, Brad, seeks out the advice of a psychic who is able to see through the eyes of Talos' victims. During Brad's consultation, the psychic sees the platform at Old Street Station and remarks that her vision seems unusually low to the ground; the next target is a guide dog. Knowing there is no time to lose, Brad dashes toward the station.

On the platform, a blind man waits with his dog for the next train. A piece of trash flutters and the dog becomes agitated, sensing the presence of Talos amid the rubbish. The dog becomes almost feral, frightening his owner and the surrounding passengers. The dog lunges toward the wrappings as Brad arrives on the platform, but he is too late; the dog is dead. When Brad rushes to the dead dog's side, the blind man mistakes him for the murderer and assaults Brad, allowing Talos' wrappings to escape and move on to their next victim.

✦   *Continue northbound on the Northern Line two stops to King's Cross St Pancras.*

Though famous for its role in the 1955 Ealing Studios comedy *The Ladykillers*, directed by Alexander Mackendrick, King's Cross Station has had a scattering of horror cameos as well. In the brilliant 1965 Amicus portmanteau movie, *Dr Terror's House of Horrors*, directed by Freddie Francis and starring Roy Castle, Peter Cushing, and Christopher Lee, the film begins with five passengers boarding a train at King's Cross Station. On the train, each passenger has their (mis)fortune read by the enigmatic Dr Schreck. In Tom Harper's *The Woman in Black 2: Angel of Death* (2014), school children gather to escape London and the Blitz during the Second World War. Leaving their families behind, the children are led by school teacher, Eve, and their headmistress, Jean. Though they feel they are doing their best for the children, they actually are moving from one horror to another, as the manor house they relocate to is haunted by the ghost made famous originally by Susan Hill's 1983 gothic horror novel, *The Woman In Black*.

It is ironic that the haunting of *Woman in Black 2* occurs after leaving the station, as King's Cross is one of the many haunted stations on the Underground network. A modern looking woman with long, brown hair is said to walk the platforms, screaming at passengers with her arms outstretched. Sightings of the woman began in the late 1980s, causing some speculation that she may have been a victim of a station fire on 18 November 1987. The fire was the worst in the history of the London Underground, killing 31 people, including an officer trying to save the trapped passengers. A memorial plaque with a clock can be seen in one of the station's interchanges, marking the date and time of the accident. Contrary to popular belief however, the clock tells the correct time, and doesn't linger morbidly on the moment of the accident's occurrence.

✦ *Change at King's Cross St Pancras for the southbound Piccadilly Line. Take the Piccadilly Line one stop to Russell Square.*

As you may remember from the Bloomsbury walk, Russell Square Station is the hunting ground for a cannibal in Gary Sherman's *Death Line* (1972). The cannibal, known only as 'Man', is the descendant of Victorian workers trapped underground when the neighbouring British Museum Station collapsed. The company who employed the workers decided against a rescue attempt because it would cost too much, leaving them for dead. Against all odds, they survived by hunting for stray passengers on the platforms of Russell Square and Holborn Stations and drinking water that leaked into the nearby mud. Man is a descendant of these people, a cannibal deformed by his subterranean life – though the film does show a human side to this monster. In the early scenes we see him using the blood of one of his victims, James Manfred OBE, to try and save his ailing, pregnant wife.

Man is only discovered when he attacks Manfred on the southbound Piccadilly Line platform of Russell Square. After a little digging, Inspector Calhoun, played by Donald Pleasence, realises that Manfred is one of at least four other disappearances at the station. For Calhoun, though, Manfred is the most important victim because of his social stature; and, as a result, Manfred's is the only case he pursues. Calhoun's prejudice echoes the same class injustice that underscored the decision to leave the trapped Victorian workers in British Museum Station. While Calhoun is no better than the Victorian company – caring more for people's rank than whether they live or die – Man is indiscriminate in his murders, killing workers, OBEs, and greengrocers regardless of background. And though Man is a cannibal, he only kills to feed himself, driven by need rather than any sentiment of revenge or class antagonism. While he is hardly a saint, a cannibal hunting through Russell Square Station is not so different, it appears, from its counterparts above ground who allow people to die without a care.

The moral ambiguity running through *Death Line* is never resolved, with the film showing the best and worst in people both above and below ground. This complex blend of good and evil is essentially how one can see the Underground portrayed in horror film: it is a nest of monsters, but also a sanctuary for hope. It forces a confrontation with uncomfortable truths like class prejudice, grief and the sins of our parents, but it also doesn't always offer easy answers or perfect solutions. The innocent are as likely to die as survive, and, as we see with Man, what can be discovered on the Underground can just as easily be buried.

Looking for More?

Many more of London's Underground and overground stations have their place in horror history. You can add any of the below horror hotspots to your route, or visit them separately if they are on your way elsewhere. Each station has a different personality in horror, a testament to the versatility of the Underground as a film location.

East Finchley Station

Transport: East Finchley
Underground Station
(Northern Line)

This out-of-the-way station appears in Nick Willing's mystic horror *Close Your Eyes* (alternatively titled *Dr Sleep*, 2002). The Underground stations in the film act as a useful mirror for the psychological work that Dr Strother does delving into dreams and the recesses of the mind. Though we don't see Strother travel much on the Underground he's usually thinking or processing his sessions as we see him exit the Tube stations, which also give a stark, procedural sense of realism to an otherwise fantastical film.

If you are able to stop off at this station, about half a mile to the west, at 37 Abbots Gardens, is the home of Shaun's mother in Edgar Wight's horror-comedy *Shaun of the Dead* (2004). Shaun, played by Simon Pegg, rescues his mother and his stepfather from the zombie hordes, but once out of the house, a hooded zombie bites Shaun's stepfather, Philip. Though the two do not get along Shaun comes to his rescue. The scene is tense but also bittersweet as Shaun wavers with the decision to take his infected stepfather with them. Philip insists that Shaun focus on his mother's safety and leave, but

Shaun decides not to leave Philip to the zombies. The act shows how much Shaun – an emotionally adolescent man-baby at the start of the film – has matured, even if his decision ultimately traps the group in a car with a man-eating zombie.

Just up the High Road from the station is one of the great old cinemas of London, the Phoenix. Having lived in East Finchley I have a great affection for it, and so does critic, writer, and horror fan Mark Kermode. Kermode is a patron of the Phoenix and regularly talks about his life-long love for the cinema, which features in *The Movie Doctors* (2015), a book he co-wrote with his radio partner Simon Mayo. This independent single screen cinema was built in 1910 and is one of the oldest continually running art-house theatres in London. The cinema has appeared on film and in television, including a brief horror cameo as the theatre in which the depressed Louis first sees a sunrise since becoming a vampire in Neil Jordan's star-studded film adaptation of Anne Rice's novel *Interview With The Vampire* (1994).

Marylebone Station

Transport: Marylebone
Underground And Rail Station
(Rail and Bakerloo Line)

Standing outside the Melcombe Place entrance to Marylebone Station, we can see the red façade and grand arched entryway is much the same as it was when it opened in 1899. This view will be familiar to anyone who has seen James Wan's *The Conjuring 2: The Enfield Case* (2016). Lorraine and Ed Warren pass through here on their way to help the Hodgson family with their resident poltergeist. As the station is about 10 miles from Enfield and does not offer a direct train service to Enfield Chase Station, its presence in the film is most likely to offer a visual hint of Gothic London to the otherwise modern ghost story.

If we walk inside the station and go straight ahead to the platforms, we can retrace the footsteps of merchant navy officer Bill Masen in Steve Sekely and Freddie Francis' adaptation of John Wyndham's vegetative horror novel, *Day of the Triffids* (1962). Having awoken at Moorfields Eye Hospital to a London blinded by a brilliant meteor shower, Masen comes to Marylebone Station hoping to get a train back to his ship in Portsmouth. As he approaches the platform a train speeds towards him, smashing dramatically into the buffers. Disoriented and panicked blind people come pouring out of the cars in the busiest scene of an otherwise abandoned London. Amid the panic, Masen encounters a schoolgirl, Susan, who has also managed to avoid being blinded by the previous night's meteor shower. As other passengers realise Susan can see, one particularly aggressive man tries to entrap Susan to act as his eyes. Masen intervenes to save her, easily avoiding the blind man's fists. From here the two of them wander empty London and make their escape to France.

As you probably already know, Marylebone Station is also just around the corner from Baker Street, fictional home to Sherlock Holmes, who made more than a few horror film appearances.

Old Aldwych Station

Transport: Temple
Underground Station
(.2 miles)

Find the red and white brickwork spelling 'Strand Station' and you've found Old Aldwych Station, the most famous of London's disused, or 'ghost', Underground stations. Formerly on the Piccadilly Line, it was used as an air raid shelter during the Blitz. Though the station closed to passengers in 1994, it has remained open to film crews, who have been using the station since the 1950s.

The disused platforms and rail lines have appeared in the guise of other stations in many horror films. They stood in for the British Museum Station and the tracks to Russell Square in *Death Line*, and the surrounding lines to Charing Cross Station in *Creep* and *28 Weeks Later*. In *Death Line* and *Creep* the underground holds secret hidden passages and rooms which house characters raised on the Underground. And the visible age of these disused spaces mirrors how decrepit the people residing there are. *Death Line*'s antagonist is visibly deformed as a result of generations of inbreeding, and the sores on his body echo his poorly maintained surroundings. In *Creep*, the once sterile medical rooms in which Craig lives –

and kills – speak of how long Craig has been abandoned to the tunnels, and of his decayed mental state.

As eerie as its platforms are on film, Old Aldwych Station itself is reputedly haunted. Workers on the Tube networks at night have regularly seen a ghost walking the tracks at the station. The ghost, a young woman, is believed to be a former actress at the nearby Royal Strand Theatre. As a result of its hauntings, the station featured in a 2002 episode of *Most Haunted*. While visiting, crackpot medium Derek Acorah claimed to have contacted the ghost, whom he called Margaret. If you want to see these otherworldly platforms for yourself, look online for open days or take a tour through Transport for London.

Dark Waters:
The Thames

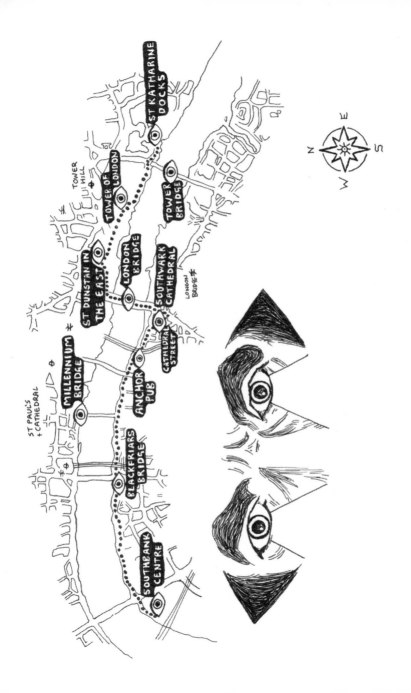

Walk Length: 2.8 miles
Starting Point:
St Katharine Docks
Transport: Tower Hill Station
(.5 miles)

End Point: Southbank Centre
Transport: Waterloo Station
(350 yards) or Embankment
Station (700 yards)

The Thames has been called the artery of the city, conveying life and energy through London and defining its landscape. Boats still zip along the river, moving tourists, freights, and even trash in and out of the capital. In horror cinema the river may not always run red with blood, but as it ebbs and flows nefarious deeds are both concealed and revealed.

Think of the Thames in horror films, and you will most likely picture a body floating in it. The first cinematic cadaver floating on the Thames was in the opening scenes of *The Dark Eyes of London* in 1939, but Alfred Hitchcock had hoped to include a scene of a body being pulled from the Thames in his 1927 silent *The Lodger: A Story of the London Fog*. Ever since, bodies have popped up from, or been dumped in, the Thames. But it is not only the dead who bob along this tidal river. Murderers and monsters have been swept up in its currents, either being welcomed into the city or cleared from its sewers. On this walk we will encounter the terrors in and around London's great river, looking at what it churns up and what it keeps hidden.

Route

✦ *Starting Point: St Katharine Docks. This is worth exploring in its own right, but begin by Thomas Telford's retracting footbridge on the south side of the docks nearest the river. If you're interested, you can read more about Telford on a plaque beside the bridge.*

In Freddie Francis' *The Creeping Flesh* (1973), Penelope Hildern, the daughter of a respected scientist played by Peter Cushing, is injected by her father with a serum in an attempt to control her madness. Instead, the medication brings out the worst in Penelope, and she breaks out of her home onto the streets of London. As she flees, she assaults several men, eventually running into an escaped asylum patient, Charles Lenny, in the warehouses across the Thames from the footbridge – now remodelled as shops and houses. The two fight, but Penelope gets the upper hand, killing Lenny with a fatal blow. Visible in the scene behind her as she attacks Lenny is Ivory House, the building behind us with a notable clocktower at the centre of the docks.

Ivory House is also the home of occult writer John Verney in another seventies horror film, Peter Sykes adaptation of Dennis Wheatley's *To The Devil ... a Daughter* (1976). Verney, played by Richard Widmark, is charged with the curious task of looking after an old friend's daughter, Catherine Beddows, who also happens to be a nun. Catherine, unbeknownst to Verney, is being pursued by the Satan-worshipping priest, Father

Michael Rayner, played by Christopher Lee. Verney brings Catherine here to his apartment where he discovers that her 18th birthday will be on All Hallows Eve, one of the sacred days in the Satanic calendar akin to a Catholic Saint's Day. Suspecting something sinister, Verney leaves Catherine in his home as he secretly tries to discover why she is in hiding.

Once Catherine is alone, Father Michael – hiding outside the city – uses his devilish powers to put Catherine into a trance and make her come to him. As Verney returns, he finds her walking the perilous waterside paths of the dock and runs after her. Father Michael seems aware of Verney, manoeuvring Catherine so that she is separated from Verney by the retracting footbridge. In desperation Verney closes the bridge by hand and sprints across the docks, removing Catherine's necklace – a gift from Father Michael – to break the trance. Having learned that Catherine is not safe alone, Verney calls on his friends to guard her and make sure she does not get lulled into another trance. Undeterred, Father Michael finds another way to possess Catherine from afar. She wakes after being sedated and stabs her minder with the handle of a comb. This time she escapes, heading for our next stop.

✦ *Walk west along St Katharine's Way, with the dock on your right and the river on your left. After 180 feet you'll come to the north end of Tower Bridge. There are stairs up to the Bridge to your right. Take the stairs up and find a quiet place to stand with a view of the bridge.*

Tower Bridge is an emblem of London throughout the world, appearing in artworks, newsreels and films across genres. In horror cinema, the bridge often acts as a visual shorthand for London, but it may also mark the gateway where terror can enter or flee the city via the Thames. This is a theme we will return to throughout the walk, but we'll focus now on films where action happens directly on the bridge.

In *To The Devil ... a Daughter*, the entranced Catherine flees Verney's apartment mentioned at our previous stop and crosses Tower Bridge. In this surreal scene, the camera appears to delve inside Catherine's altered mental state, using a fisheye lens to distort the perspective and have the bridge seemingly bend around her. In one shot traffic causes the camera to sway, making her walk appear even more precarious, and accentuating the danger she faces under Father Michael's control. As she walks across the bridge and then past the Tower of London, she takes her last, hurried steps out of the city.

Tower Bridge in many horror films marks a villain or anti-hero's entry into London. In Tim Burton's retelling of *Sweeney Todd: The Demon Barber of Fleet Street* (2007) the bridge rises to welcome Todd as he enters the city, sinisterly singing the song 'No Place Like London'. The song is a vivid indictment of corruption at the heart of London, and Todd spits every line at the city in disgust. He returns a wronged man, bent on avenging himself after a corrupt Judge destroyed his family. In both Eugène Lourié and Douglas Hickox's *Behemoth the Sea Monster* (1959) and Lourié's own *Gorgo* (1961), gigantic monsters encounter Tower Bridge in scenes that mark their first attacks on London. In *Gorgo*, Tower Bridge does not survive the encounter: Gorgo's mother, a colossal lizard, first takes down the south tower with her claws, halting the military defensive action, before moving onto the suspension bridge and remaining tower. Bodies fall into the Thames as an onlooking newscaster declares: 'one of London's oldest landmarks, smashed like matchsticks'. It is the first of many failed attempts by the military to keep London safe. In *Behemoth The Sea Monster* the Bridge remains intact while the Behemoth, an aquatic dinosaur identified by the film's Professor Bickford as a Paleosaurus, comes ashore for the first time attacking the docks before emitting a burst of radiation that would kill any survivors.

In Stephen Sommers' *The Mummy Returns* (2001), the bridge's moving bascules provide a further frisson of danger. After saving Evie from vengeful mummies at the British Museum, Rick and his family bolt in an old London General red double-decker bus, with the mummies and members of an Egyptian cult in pursuit. When they cross Tower Bridge, having destroyed the last of the mummies, the bus runs out of fuel. Evie and Rick get out of the bus along with their son Alex, but are unable to prevent unseen members of the cult kidnapping him. The kidnappers flee across Tower Bridge, raising the bridge behind them. In an action scene familiar from countless films, a despairing Rick jumps the widening gap and manages to grab hold of the other side, only to see the men drive off with his son.

Tower Bridge provides a fitting location for a gang robbery at the outset of John Llewellyn Moxey's *Circus Of Fear* (1966). After attacking an armoured vehicle, the gang lower their bounty onto a boat waiting below and escape upriver. When the leader of the gang goes to dispose of a vehicle used in the heist he is killed by an unseen knife-thrower, a masked man working at a local circus.

In a rare moment of joy, in Juan Carlos Fresnadillo's *28 Weeks Later* (2007), siblings Tammy and Andy break quarantine and speed over the empty Tower Bridge on a stolen motorcycle. Having previously been kept abroad for years by the terrifying Rage virus, the two decide to escape a quarantine zone maintained by the US military and visit their family home. As anyone who has been through the recent Covid lockdown can understand, the temptation of freedom when on lockdown can be great, but the risks were even greater. Just as we had to stay home to keep the virus from spreading, Tammy and Andy risk the lives of everyone in quarantine when their trip reveals a surviving Rage victim: their mother.

✦ *Retrace your steps down the stairs and then follow the short foot tunnel under Tower Bridge. Continue along the riverside path with the Tower of London on your right. This stretch of the embankment is often busy, but try and find a quiet place to stand and look at the Tower.*

As a landmark of London, the Tower makes brief appearances in John Landis' *An American Werewolf in London* (1981) and Alan Gibson's *The Satanic Rites of*

Dracula (1973). It also has a minor presence in Piers Haggard's *The Fiendish Plot of Dr Fu Manchu* (1980), a film based on the notorious Chinese criminal overlord of Sax Rohmer's 'yellow peril' fiction. After Dr Fu Manchu's organisation steal a rare diamond, The Star of Leningrad, Scotland Yard seek out retired police officer (and Fu's nemesis), Sir Denis Nayland Smith, played by Peter Sellers. Smith suspects Fu Manchu will also try to steal the diamond's twin, housed in the Tower of London. Nayland realises the Tower of London is too heavily protected – a moment made comical by showing the aged Beefeaters standing guard – and concludes that Fu Manchu will attempt to kidnap the Queen instead.

As mentioned in the previous stop, a possessed young nun passes by the Tower of London on her way to Christopher Lee's ghoulish Father Michael in *To The Devil ... a Daughter*. The path Catherine takes in her trance makes no sense in real life: she leaves St Katharine's Dock and crosses Tower Bridge, but finds herself at the north side of the Tower of London (which, as we've seen, is on the same side of the river as the dock). This surreal route is disorienting and helps disconnect Catherine – and the audience – from reality. It also ensures the final image of Catherine in London is next to a medieval structure famed for its executions, anticipating the ancient ritual Father Michael will perform with Catherine at the uniquely hexagonal Dashwood Mausoleum in High Wycombe. The Dashwood Mausoleum is named for the English politician Francis Dashwood, Chancellor of the Exchequer (1762-1763) and co-founder of the

Hellfire Club, a private members club known for its pagan, usually Bacchanalian, events. Though neither are mentioned in the film, this pagan connection ties in well with Father Michael performing a pagan ritual at the heart of Dashwood's mausoleum.

In a more positive take on the location, both Tower Bridge and the Tower of London lend a sense of hope to the final scene of Matthias Hoene's *Cockneys vs Zombies* (2012). A hodgepodge mix of family and friends from the East End escape the zombie hordes overtaking London by jumping onto a boat. As they float past the two landmarks, military planes fly overhead, and they wonder if London can survive. The grandfather of two of the survivors, Ray, makes a rousing speech insisting London will survive because of its people. Seeing Tower Bridge and the Tower of London, both of which survived world changing events and two world wars, bolsters Ray's argument: London has and always will survive.

Beyond the realm of cinema, the Tower itself is widely believed to be the most haunted building in London. The collection of ghosts include the spirit of Archbishop of Canterbury Thomas Becket – murdered a little further afield in Canterbury Cathedral in 1170 – and that of Anne Boleyn, the beheaded wife of portly monarch Henry VIII. While the murders of both Becket and Boleyn have been startlingly captured by harrowing film and television productions, their spectres have yet to make it onto the big screen. Perhaps their time will come?

✦ *Continue along the riverside path. When you reach the Tower Millennium Pier on your left, turn right. Pass the Tower of London gift shop and turn left on to Lower Thames Street. Continue for 175 yards, with a large dual carriageway joining from the right. Cross this at the pedestrian crossing, then turn right and walk along to the junction with St Dunstan's Hill. Turn left and walk up St Dunstan's Hill towards the ruined church of St Dunstan in the East. If the garden is open, go in and find a quiet place to stop – perhaps near the fountain in the roofless nave of the church.*

This atmospheric, ruined church – originally built in 1100, but modified by Christopher Wren following the Great Fire of London – was heavily damaged during the Blitz. The ruined exterior of the church now exists as a public peace garden, startlingly reclaimed by nature. Its tangled vines and creeping horticulture may even remind some readers of John Wyndham's Triffids. The site became a shelter for the super-intelligent telekinetic children of Anton Leader's *Children of the Damned* (1964). When the children realise their respective governments intend to use their powers to spy on one another, they escape and hide here with the help of one child's aunt, Susan. Fearing the children's telekinetic abilities could be used against them, the government assume the children are using the church as a bunker from which to attack. Dr Tom Lewellin, who is leading a study on the children, tries to negotiate peacefully, but when the children realise two soldiers are preparing to burst in, they use their powers to force one man to shoot the other and then leap from the balcony to his death.

The standoff escalates from there until, in one of the most touching endings to a horror film, the children beg the army to be left alone where they can be safe. The government responds by destroying the church with explosives. We see the steeple of St Dunstan collapse in on itself as the children are killed – an uncanny echo of the near-destruction of the church in the Blitz.

✦ *Retrace your steps down St Dunstan's Hill and back across Lower Thames Street. The most direct route to the next stop is to continue along Lower Thames Street for 350 yards, then climb the steps on your left to London Bridge.*

Sometimes confused by visitors for Tower Bridge, London Bridge offers one of the best river views in the city. Straight ahead we can glimpse the chilling corporate spectacle of Renzo Piano's Shard and the tower of Southwark Cathedral, near to which Thomas Becket would have stayed before his ill-fated pilgrimage to Canterbury; to the right, the heart of the ancient City of London along the curve of the Thames; and to the left is the first stop we visited on this walk: the ominous Tower of London.

In Walter Summers' *The Dark Eyes of London* (1939), we see Tower Bridge from this distant vantage point as the opening credits roll and traffic passes along the bridge. After a heartbeat, two looming eyes fade in at the centre of the Bridge. The eyes glare through the luminous screen, growing until they completely overtake the bridge. The eyes floating over Tower Bridge recognisably belong to Bela Lugosi, still famous at the time for his role in Universal's *Dracula* (1931), who stars in this film as Dr Orloff. The frightening image hints that Orloff's evil has truly gripped the city before the film even begins, as we eventually discover that he has been drowning victims of his insurance scam and using the Thames to make their murders appear as accidents. In the end, though, the river betrays him. On closer inspection of the water in one victim's lungs, police discover that the water is too clean to have come from the polluted Thames. Before the police can arrest him, Orloff is thrown from his balcony in a scuffle and, in a final act of poetic justice, drowns in the river.

Similarly, in Hugo Fregonese's *Man in the Attic* (1953) the Thames helps the Ripper-like Slade, played by Jack Palance, wash his hands of blood and clean the murder weapon throughout the film. In the final moments however, the river turns on him: when Slade jumps into the Thames to escape the police, he drowns. *Man in the Attic* was based on the novel *The Lodger* by Marie Belloc Lowndes, and the book would also inspire John Brahm's adaptation, *The Lodger*, in 1944. Brahm's film also shows the police chase the murderous Slade to the Thames, where he jumps into the river and is carried away by the current. Police inspector Warwick and the heroine, Kitty, go down to the embankment in the hope of finding Slade's body. With Tower Bridge behind them, they agree that that the river has carried Slade away; in Warwick's words, the Thames has '[swept] the city clean'.

The Thames is a common feature of London horror films, but despite Warwick's description of it as a solution to a murderous problem, it's function is never really fixed. Oftentimes the river is characterised by its capacity for secrecy. In *Frenzy* (1972), *Madhouse* (1974), and *Vampire Diary* (2006) for example, the victim's bodies are found in the Thames, the river having washed away any evidence of the murderer. In Douglas Hickox's *Theatre of Blood* (1973), the Thames clandestinely keeps a person alive: when actor Edward Lionheart leaps to his death in the Thames from the riverside apartment of his most scathing critic, he is washed ashore in the Thames estuary, where he is revived by vagrants who help him seek revenge.

In a humorous take on the river and its secrets in Herbert J. Leder's *It!* (1967) museum curator Pimm devises an ingenious solution to the problem of an increasingly unruly golem by telling it to stand at the bottom of the Thames. Unfortunately for him, Pimm has lost some of his control over the golem, and it appears in his museum the next day, dripping wet. As you pass over the river consider what may be lying below the waves of the Thames now, just waiting to pop up.

✦ *Continue across London Bridge and over the Thames. When you reach the far side, cross the bridge road at the first crossing, then turn right. On your left you'll see a road running beneath this road, and just past it there's*

a set of steps. Go down the steps and turn right on to
Montague Close. Walk along Montague Close for fifty
yards, to a small riverside park with trees. Stand with
your back to the river and look at the imposing foursquare
tower of Southwark Cathedral.

In Bob Clark's old-fashioned Ripper-Holmes horror
mash-up *Murder By Decree* (1979) Holmes comes to
Southwark Cathedral – once the medieval priory church
of St Mary Overie – for the funeral of murdered sex
worker Catherine Eddowes. Holmes searches the crowd
around the cathedral for Mary Kelly, whom he knows
to be the Ripper's true target. When Mary glimpses
Holmes she runs, but he's able to catch up with her in a
nearby alley. Mary quickly tells Holmes that in order to
solve the case of the Ripper he needs to find her friend,
Annie Crook, in an asylum. As they part, Mary is seized
and pulled into a demonic black carriage, which nearly
runs Holmes down as it races off.

These backstreets were also the location of an eerie
chase in Robert Pratten's indie horror *Mindflesh* (2008).
Most of the film takes place in this area, lending a
sense of the real, less recognisable, London to this
otherwise surreal, Cronenbergian film. A cabbie, Chris
Jackson, begins to have ominous dreams and visions,
and the world of his mind becomes the true playing
field of the film. In these streets Jackson encounters
a doctor who insists, cryptically, that his visions have
angered supreme entities called 'The Guardians'. To
escape them, he must 'release their goddess from his

mind,' although the doctor does not explain how this might be possible.

✦ *Continue along Montague Close as it curves left. Walk past the west end of Southwark Cathedral on to Cathedral Street. This area can be exceptionally crowded when Borough Market (straight ahead) is open, so if the gates of the cathedral churchyard are open go in. Find a quiet place to stop with a view of the giant glasshouses of the market.*

In another Ripper/Holmes crossover, James Hill's *A Study in Terror* (1965), Dr Murray, a young physician, addresses a growing mob concerned with the Ripper murders here on Cathedral Street. Despite Murray's attempts to quell the fear in the crowd, the people of the area are so frightened that they demand mob justice. This reflects the state of popular feeling during the original period of the Ripper murders: some of the poorer citizens of Whitechapel took matters into their own hands, agreeing that the police were not genuinely interested in protecting them. Some Ripper theorists have argued that the murderer fled the city fearing this mob justice, though in the film the mob has no effect on the Ripper, who, it is revealed, does not even live in London.

On the way to the next stop we will pass through Clink Street, where police finally corner the werewolf, David, in *An American Werewolf in London*. In the film, David's werewolf form runs wild in the West End when he is cornered by the police, meaning the scene should have been filmed miles from Clink Street. However, the quieter Southbank area offered an ideal shooting location with a street wide enough to accommodate the several police cars which corner the werewolf (in addition to the film crew). Once the werewolf is trapped, David's girlfriend, Alex, steps between the police and David. Appealing to the man within the monster, she confesses that she loves him. The words seem to reach David, but only in time for the police to shoot him, making this street both a literal and metaphorical dead end in the film.

✦ *Return to Cathedral Street and turn right. Follow the road as it forks to the left, passing the Golden Hinde – a replica of Sir Francis Drake's flagship – on your right. Near the entrance to the Golden Hinde turn left on to Pickfords' Wharf. Continue along Pickfords' Wharf as it becomes Clink Street, passing the medieval ruins of Winchester Palace and (further on) The Clink Prison. Pass under a large railway bridge to the junction with Bank End. Turn right and follow Bank End to the south bank of the Thames and the Anchor pub. Again, this area can be busy, so try and find a quiet place to stop – possibly in the Anchor's outdoor seating area.*

Sitting among the outdoor seats here between the Cannon Street Railway Bridge and Southwark Bridge, hypnotherapist Dr Michael Strother and his patient, police officer Janet Losey learn about the long-deceased occultist Francis Paladine and his modern practitioners in Nick Willing's *Close Your Eyes* (2002). When treating Janet for hypnotherapy, Strother gets a psychic vision of a girl within Janet's mind. The girl has been kidnapped and is found later, unable to speak and with tattoos on her body. Janet convinces Strother to help in her investigation, leading them down a supernatural path to track down the notorious 'Tattoo Killer' within Paladine's cult and expose their attempt to manipulate human souls.

✦ *Continue along the riverside path, through a foot tunnel under Southwark Bridge and past Shakespeare's Globe. In 260 yards you'll reach the Millennium Bridge in front of the Tate Modern. Take the stairs up to the bridge, but don't cross it – just look across the river to St Paul's Cathedral.*

The Millennium Bridge makes a brief appearance in *28 Weeks Later* as a cluster of infected rush across the bridge toward St Paul's. The Rage-infected zombies are led by Don, the father of Tammy and Andy, who brought the Rage infection into the quarantine zone. The shot confirms that the infected have reclaimed London, and that they are in hot pursuit of the survivors.

St Paul's Cathedral, on the other side of the river, is another common feature of London horror films, dominating the London skyline in Victorian horrors like *From Hell* or simply establishing a location, as in the final scenes of Tony Scott's *The Hunger* (1983) (see the St Paul's Cathedral hotspot). Just a glimpse of the cathedral can send a powerful message, as it does in *Day of the Triffids*. After Susan and Bill Masen discover a car amid the deserted streets of London, they drive off for France; the dome of St Paul's is behind them, rising above swirls of smoke as flames lick the buildings below. This image recalls one of the most famous images of the London Blitz: 'St Paul's survives', taken after a bombing raid in December 1940 and published on the front page of the *Daily Mail*. In the photograph, the dome stands tall above the smoke of the bombed city, a symbol of wartime triumph and British endurance. By mimicking the famous photograph, the scene immediately evokes a battered London, but the mood in the film is dark rather than hopeful, as two survivors abandon the city rather than remaining to preserve it.

✦ *Continue along the riverside path for 350 yards, passing the entrance to Blackfriars Station under Blackfriars Railway Bridge, and a foot tunnel decorated with tiles under Blackfriars Bridge. Stop just after Blackfriars Bridge, opposite the oddly shaped Doggett's Coat and Badge pub, and turn back towards the bridge.*

Blackfriars Bridge was the subject of one of the earliest films made in London. In 1896 British film pioneer R.W. Paul set up his camera on the southside of the bridge looking north and filmed the movement of people and carriages over the bridge. Today, the bridge is visible in a wide variety of films from Charles Crichton's Ealing comedy *The Lavender Hill Mob* (1951) to Christopher McQuarrie's *Mission: Impossible – Fallout* (2018).

For the horror cinema fan, the most memorable image of the bridge comes in Danny Boyle's *28 Days Later*, where an insignificant protagonist walks across the Thames in a deserted London, heading into the City. Shot from a great distance, Jim looks trivial beside the large buildings and broad, empty bridges over the river. The scene gives one the sense that London has always been out of proportion with the people who inhabit it. The rebuilding of Blackfriars Station has changed the look of the bridge and the view, but the vista towards St Paul's is still recognisable.

Just across the river from here is roughly the spot where a badly burned young man jumps into the Thames in Terence Fisher's *Phantom of the Opera* (1962). In this London-based twist on the original story, an aspiring opera composer, Professor Petrie, takes his first complete opera to the famous Lord Ambrose D'Arcy for his notes. Ambrose tells Petrie the opera is terrible, but later publishes it under his own name. When Petrie discovers the deception, he goes to the printing press in Farringdon with the intention of burning the manuscripts, only to set fire to the building, igniting himself in the process. Severely burned, he races to the Thames and flings himself in. The police insist that Petrie died in the incident, but when producer Harry Hunter investigates, the sound of music coming up from the river suggests that Petrie may still be alive as the Phantom of the Opera. The film condenses and rearranges the geography of the city, but the idea the Phantom could live in tunnels accessible to the river was inspired by the many archways and outlets along this stretch left open for rivers to drain into the Thames.

✦ *Continue Along the Thames Path past Gabriel's Wharf. After 520 yards, you will pass under Waterloo Bridge; the Southbank Centre is on your left.*

The brutalist architecture of the Southbank Centre becomes a strange maze in Peter Collinson's *Straight On Till Morning* (1972). Among its various levels and walkways the shy, naïve Brenda notices her crush, Peter, looking for his dog. When she finds the dog, she decides to kidnap it briefly in order to get Peter's attention, but not before he witnesses her do it. After cleaning the scruffy dog, and getting herself into a nice outfit, she returns the dog to Peter using the address on its collar. Peter surprises Brenda by demanding to know why she took it and when she confesses her attraction, he unexpectedly asks her to move in with him. Once she leaves, Peter stabs the dog; a small taste of his plans for Brenda. Peter has a murderous response to anything conventionally pretty, even his newly cleaned dog. The cold concrete façades and shadowy under crofts of the Southbank Centre seem to suit his austere and unforgiving personality.

Sci-fi television has also taken advantage of the brutalist Southbank Centre. It has served as a futuristic world in the eleventh episode of season two of *Blake's*

7 (1978-1981) and a dystopian landscape in *Philip K Dick's Electric Dreams* (2017-2018). The basement was transformed into a prison in the *Dr Who* episode 'Frontier in Space' (aired 1973), while the once-industrialised riverside site also appeared in an early murder mystery film, *Three Cases of Murder* (1955), directed by Wendy Toye, George More O'Ferrall, and David Eady. On summer nights you can enjoy outdoor screenings of films here, including horror films – an enjoyable date night, if you're not Brenda.

As a final image in our journey along the river, on 29 August 1971 the body of Alfred Hitchcock was seen floating a little further up the Thames, just beyond Hungerford Bridge. The body was peacefully bobbing, face up, his hands folded over his chest. This was not the man himself, but a dummy used to film the trailer for his 1972 horror *Frenzy*. Floating past Jubilee Gardens, it caused quite a stir for onlookers and provided a fantastic shot for local newspapers – not to say extra publicity for *Frenzy*. It is also something of a fitting memorial to the cinematic role of the Thames in horror by one of London's native horror directors.

Looking for More?

While the Thames plays a varied role in horror, many of the stories along its banks include themes of invasion. Tower Bridge, a symbolic entrance to the city, is attacked by giant monsters in both *Gorgo* and *Behemoth the Sea Monster* and, once past the bridge, they lay waste to the rest of the city. At St Dunstan's in the East, the ominously talented and cerebral 'Children of the Damned' are attacked by the army as though they are an invading force. On Bankside, a psychiatrist and a police officer discuss their dreams being invaded, while on the bridges the zombie-like infected run wild. But such a large city has many opportunities for invasion, including these horror hotspots outside the city's centre:

Kew Gardens

Transport: Kew Bridge Rail Station (.7 miles)

Kew Gardens Underground Station (.9 miles)

The ornate botanic glass houses of Kew are worth a trip in their own right, but when you come to the Palm House take a moment to pause and remember the Triffids. In Steve Sekely and Freddie Francis' *Day of the Triffids* (1962) the Palm House contains samples of the Triffid plant, which turn monstrous on the night of a great meteor shower. Lights flash in the sky while a guard makes his rounds through the Palm House. When he settles down to his packed lunch, he is attacked from behind by a looming mobile Triffid. As it turns out, the shower has blinded all those who saw it, allowing the man-eating Triffids to overtake the human population. This first kill sets the tone for the rest of the film, as the Triffids' unique noises and tentacled appendages become more dangerous than the accident-prone blindness itself.

The nearby Steam Museum is the site of a visually spectacular chase in Stephen Weeks' *I, Monster* (1971). This period horror took inspiration from Robert Louis Stevenson's *The Strange Case of Dr Jekyll and Mr Hyde*, as psychologist Charles Marlowe tests a drug to release inhibitions, unintentionally bringing forth the evil within himself. As his evil persona, Edward Blake, he becomes hideous and for this reason is rejected by sex worker, Annie, in a pub. When Annie leaves work for the night, Blake pursues her in a chase across the city and through the Thames Waterworks. Though actually filmed in Kempton Steam Museum further west, much of the same equipment can be seen in the London Museum of Water and Steam, close to Kew Bridge. The Museum is well worth a visit in its own right, and gives a sense of the dramatic large-scale steam structures you see in the film. Blake and Annie play cat and mouse among the heaving machines and spinning wheels. The site is spectacular, threatening both their lives, but in the end, Blake corners her after she exits the museum onto a narrow alleyway. Annie gives in, thinking Blake wants her virtue, but he takes her life instead, leaving behind a bloodied cane that will eventually lead to his capture.

Crouch End:
A Mini-Walk

Transport: Harringay Rail
Station (.6 miles)
Hornsey Rail Station
(.6 miles)

Crouch Hill Overground
Station (.9 miles)

As you walk to the heart of Crouch End from one of the
nearby stations, you'll have a good sense of the pleasant,
average neighbourhood which defines North London
horror films. Suburban houses, gardens and schools
represent a mundane reality that horror films delight
in disturbing. Number 83 Nelson Road – the location of
Shaun's flat in Edgar Wright's *Shaun of the Dead* (2004)
– is exactly this kind of familiar London nowhere.

Here, we see inside Shaun's life, caught between
his lazy and non-rent paying best friend, Ed, and his
responsible and irritable roommate, Pete. This is also
where Shaun and Ed encounter a zombie in the garden,
which they kill by flinging old vinyl records at it. In this
famous scene, the slow pace of the zombie gives Shaun
and Ed plenty of time to decide what records are worth the
sacrifice. Though the zombie threat has been building
gradually for some time, this confrontation makes
Shaun realise that he and everyone he cares about are in

danger. Sitting in their front room, Shaun and Ed come up with a plan to save Shaun's ex-girlfriend and mother. Initially their plan includes coming back to the flat, but with the garden window broken the Winchester pub becomes the safer option. Before leaving, they discover the flat is even less safe than they imagined: Pete has become a zombie. Rather than kill his roommate, Shaun leaves him trapped in the bathroom, while he and Ed escape in Pete's car.

Before this, Shaun is completely oblivious to the growing zombie invasion, made clear in two scenes where Shaun walks from his home to the local grocer at 96 Weston Park to get a cornetto. The two scenes take place before and after zombies have taken over Shaun's neighbourhood and are filmed nearly identically, including Shaun tripping on the lip of the pavement as he comes to the store, but on the second walk, Shaun is ignoring signs of danger behind him. For example, on his first journey to the store he passes by a man washing his car and on the second walk the car's windshield is shattered. Once in the store, Shaun fails to notice two bloody handprints streaking the chiller-cabinet door as he gets a Diet Coke. He then slips on something (most likely blood) on his way to grab a cornetto and leaves money on the counter, unaware of the zombified store owner, Nelson, behind him.

As Shaun lives in Crouch End, we see more of its streets and shops in the film. He speaks with a friend, Yvonne, on Farrer Road, and buys his mother flowers from a shop at number 10 on the Broadway across from the park. But if you took Park Road out of the centre of Crouch End for a mile, you would find yourself at 54 Duke's Avenue in Muswell Hill where the Paul Andrew Williams' horror thriller *Cherry Tree Lane* (2010) was filmed. This home invasion horror relied on the contrast between a peaceful leafy neighbourhood exterior and the torture and terror within the house. Cherry Tree Lane is also a reference to the studio-created Disney street on which *Mary Poppins* was filmed – another way of heightening the difference between the appearance of a perfectly ordered suburban community and the dark reality behind the polished front doors. If home invasion isn't up your street, you can continue along Crouch End Hill until it divides and take Hornsey Lane to Highgate Cemetery. This horror hotspot is only a mile away and well worth linking with Crouch End for an afternoon's exploration.

London Zoo

Transport: Camden Town
Underground Station (1 mile)   Prince Albert Road / London
Zoo Bus Stop (.7 miles)

A day at the zoo may not strike fear in anyone's heart, but London Zoo has made an appearance in a scattering of horror films, beginning with Stuart Walker's *Werewolf of London* (1935). Botanist Wilfred Glendon turns into a werewolf by night. One such evening he heads to the Zoo and releases a wolf before attacking a guard who he discovers is having an affair. The zoo animals go wild when they encounter the werewolf Glendon, scenting danger while also recognising him as one of their own.

In a twist on this scene over forty years later, in John Landis' *An American Werewolf in London* (1981) David awakens in the wolf enclosure of London Zoo unable to remember how he spent the night before. Adding to his predicament, David is completely naked. Embarrassed and confused, David hides in a hedge while trying to convince a child to give him clothes. He ultimately steals a woman's bright pink coat, so he can leave with some of his dignity.

London Zoo also appeared in Val Guest's early Hammer hit *The Quatermass Xperiment* (1955) when the sickly astronaut Carroon hides from searching authorities in the London Zoo. As Carroon makes his way through the zoo, the animals all panic as they sense the alien energy within him. Carroon's disease is actually an alien force within his body that sucks the life from anything it comes in contact with, taking on some of its physical properties. By morning the zoo is strewn with the animal carcasses of such victims. Amongst the debris, Dr Bernard Quatermass discovers some unidentified matter – which turns out to be a piece of Carroon – that he takes back to his lab. After careful examination, Quatermass discovers the truth of Carroon's alien identity and surmises that it is consuming animals and plants at a rate that could destroy every living thing in Britain.

More recently, London Zoo also makes an appearance in the Francis Ford Coppola's pantomimic *Bram Stoker's Dracula* (1992). Dracula visits the Zoo and takes a wolf under his spell which he then unleashes on London. The Zoo appears in both the book and the film, making use of the novelty of the zoo at the time Stoker was writing. For late-nineteenth-century Londoners, the zoo was a marvel of unusual and rarely seen animals, making them as exotic and unpredictable as the vampire to the reader. Dracula's control represents a control over the animal within himself, a struggle for David with his were-self and represented by Carroon's human/alien monster. In horror cinema, London Zoo seems to elucidate the dangerous beast that might dwell within us all.

Beneath the
Skin of History:
The East End

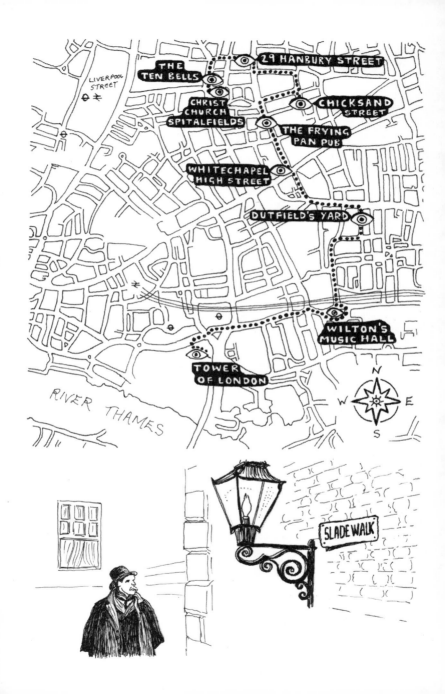

Walk Length: 2.2 miles

Starting Point: Ten Bells Pub

Transport: Liverpool Street
Station, or Aldgate East
Station (both 520 yards)

End Point: Tower of London

Transport: Tower Hill Station

Cobbled streets, tendrils of brown fog, the hazy glow of a gas lamp: filmmakers don't need much more than these simple elements to evoke the Victorian East End. This handful of visual cues appear repeatedly in horror, especially in films which draw on the history and mythology of Jack the Ripper, from Alfred Hitchcock's *The Lodger: A Story of the London Fog* (1927) to the Hughes Brothers' *From Hell* (2001). The famous serial killer murdered at least five women in Whitechapel from August to September of 1888, gruesomely mutilating several of his victims' bodies. As he was never caught – though the murders did stop – the mystery of the Ripper captured the popular imagination, and still inspires books, films and television shows offering solutions to who the Ripper was and why his killings stopped as suddenly as they started.

The Blitz, post-war decline, urban regeneration and the springboard of contemporary art have transformed the East End in the hundred and thirty odd years since the Ripper's bloody reign, but on screen the area has hardly changed. Even off screen, tourists still flock to Whitechapel so they can follow the footsteps of the Ripper murders, often to the disappointment of local residents. We're going to explore this story from a broader cinematic angle, but as we go, we'll discover that even the most recent films set in the modern East End draw on the rich history of the area. The East End, more than any other part of on-screen London it would appear, is haunted by its past.

Route

✦ *Starting Point: the Ten Bells Pub. If you decide to visit the pub, be sure to take a look at the painted tile mural inside. It depicts Spitalfields as it was at the time of the Ripper.*

The Ten Bells Pub is a centrepiece of Ripper lore. Some witnesses reported that two of his victims – Annie Chapman and Mary Jane Kelly – drank at the pub before their murders. Mary was also known to pick up her clients from outside the pub, and some drinkers claim to have seen Annie's ghost sitting at the bar on quiet nights.

Because of this connection it features as a meeting place for the Ripper's victims in The Hughes Brothers' *From Hell* (2001). At the Ten Bells, we see the women picking up their clients, gather for a rest and even discuss how to keep themselves safe from Jack the Ripper. Their fears are well-founded as the Ripper picks up Annie just outside the pub, but it still does not keep them from meeting here. Because of its importance to these women, the lead inspector on the case, Frederick Abberline, goes to the Ten Bells after the final murder looking for a message from one of the girls he happens to have fallen in love with, Mary Kelly. *From Hell* was actually shot in Prague, but the CGI and set recreation of the Ten Bells in the film is surprisingly accurate from the outside, even retaining the distinctive columns around the entry door.

The well-known connection between the Ripper's victims and the Ten Bells has made it part of many Ripper-inspired horror films. It appeared or was referenced in Monty Berman and Robert S. Baker's *Jack The Ripper* (1959), James Hill's *A Study In Terror* (1965), and Bob Clark's *Murder By Decree* (1979), and is somewhat alluded to with the pub murder in Roy Ward Baker's *Dr Jekyll and Sister Hyde* (1971). In *Dr Jekyll and Sister Hyde*, Dr Jekyll discovers how to prolong his life using female pituitary glands. When he runs out of cadavers for his experiments, he decides to commit murder, but his conscience ultimately refuses. At this point, his increasingly powerful female identity, Edwina Hyde, decides to take matters into her own hands. She waits outside a pub for a working girl to emerge and brutally kills her, removing her glands in the street. The murder outside the pub is clearly modelled on Jack the Ripper but exists in a parallel world constructed by the film rather than offering a true retelling of the murders. The pub, though actually called the 'The Old Swan' in the film, has a similar façade to the Ten Bells.

✦ *Turn around. Directly across Commercial Street is Christ Church Spitalfields.*

The gates of Christ Church across from the Ten Bells set the scene in the opening to the Holmes/Ripper crossover *A Study in Terror*, but it was far more important to the Ripper story of Alan Moore and Eddie Campbell's graphic novel, *From Hell*, on which the 2001 film was based. Christ Church Spitalfields, built by Nicholas Hawksmoor, is a feature of the graphic novel due to its supposed Masonic links. If you have been on the Bloomsbury walk or to the St Paul's Cathedral hotspot, you'll know that in Moore's story the Ripper is a Mason and a doctor, and his murders are inspired by Masonic power. Hawksmoor and his mentor Christopher Wren were believed to be Freemasons, and in some bodies of conspiratorial and literary thought, were said to have built churches on locations which might concentrate a form of cosmic male power. Before Moore published *From Hell*, Hawksmoor's churches – already associated with Freemasonry – were linked with both human sacrifice and arcane thought thanks to Peter Ackroyd's 1985 novel *Hawksmoor* and Iain Sinclair's prose poem odyssey of 1975, *Lud Heat*. Ackroyd's novel suggests that an 18th century architect (named Dyer in the book) uses eight of the churches he constructs, including Christ Church, to perform Satanic human sacrifices. The novel demonstrates the ritualistic power and concentrated energies associated with Hawksmoor and his imposing churches, which is also harnessed by *From Hell*.

Returning to the film, the famous spire is less significant to the Ripper murders, but still provides an ominous presence. In *From Hell*'s opening scene we see Mary Kelly below the spire talking with one of her friends and surveying the area for clients. The church's grand architecture seems somewhat out of place amid such devastating poverty and degradation. Later in the film, the Queen's grandson Prince Edward walks the streets of the East End in disguise. Before the murders began, Edward used to frequent the neighbourhood under the name Albert Sickert, and fell in love with one of Kelly's friends, Ann Crook, who has recently been kidnapped. The camera follows Edward (possibly looking for Ann or her friends) walking in front of the church in the fog as bells ring out. The well-dressed Edward is obviously an incongruous presence among the desperate poor – one of whom shakes violently with cold or illness before the church steps. Edward is approached by a sex worker and cowers, before diving into a carriage driven by Netley, the coachman who helps Jack the Ripper procure his victims.

✦ *Walk north along Commercial Street with Christ Church behind you on your right, and take the next right on to Hanbury Street. Number 29 is on your left, marked by a graffiti covered door in the side of Old Truman Brewery.*

The second victim of Jack the Ripper, Annie Chapman, was found dead in a yard at 29 Hanbury Street, which has since been built over by this brewery. Chapman was poor and rented a room by the day in a nearby lodging house. On the night of the murder she did not have quite enough money and returned to the streets to obtain the remaining sum. Her body was discovered in the early hours of the morning, and the police swiftly connected it with the first victim, Mary Ann Nichols, establishing the theory of a serial killer before the Ripper got his name.

Though this location is not recreated on film, Annie Chapman's death is essential to the plot in two Jack the

Ripper movies. In *A Study in Terror*, Sherlock Holmes insists on being allowed to see Annie Chapman's body, despite the protests of Inspector Lestrade. Holmes only manages to convince the inspector by suggesting another murder is to come, and Holmes may be able to prevent it. The marks on her corpse suggest Chapman was attacked by two weapons, one of which Holmes identifies as a surgeon's scalpel. This detail helps Holmes narrow suspects to someone with medical knowledge. While examining the body, Holmes also meets a Dr Murray, who is performing the autopsy and ends up being a vital link in the case when Holmes discovers that Murray's associate, Michael, married an intended victim of the Ripper.

In *From Hell*, Annie Chapman is picked up by Netley – the same coachman we saw Edward use in the last stop – outside the Ten Bells. When her dead body is discovered, Inspector Abberline gets a vision of Annie's murder the night before. As he examines the crime scene, he also notices a recurring clue: Annie is holding a stalk from a clump of grapes. This leads Abberline to insist the killer must be a man of wealth, a line of enquiry everyone else in the police force vehemently denies, either through prejudice or conspiracy. It turns out that Abberline is correct, and that the police commissioner, Charles Warren, has known so all along. Warren, like the Ripper, is a Mason and hiding the connection between the murders and the Royal family. Throughout the investigation, Warren tries to thwart Abberline, even threatening his job. Abberline is undeterred, not least because he genuinely cares about the victims. As a sign of respect not otherwise shown to these women, he leaves coins on Annie's eyes to pay 'the Ferryman' taking her to the afterlife.

✦ *Continue along Hanbury Street, following it round to the right at the junction with Spital Street. At the junction with Spelman Street turn right and walk down to the junction with Chicksand Street. Chicksand Street Park is on your right.*

Moving away from the Ripper murders, Chicksand Street is one of many locations where Dracula sends six boxes of soil from his English home, Carfax Abbey, in Bram Stoker's 1897 novel *Dracula*. Dracula brought this soil with him from Transylvania so he could bury himself and rest peacefully at night. The six boxes of soil in Chicksand Street will allow Dracula to create one of these resting places in the East End, a location chosen because it was a working-class area of London when the book came out, associated with both immigration and crime. The fear of immigration weighs heavily in *Dracula*: the Count is an immigrant who, with each step he makes to integrate himself in Britain, threatens the lives of its citizens.

This location would also have resonated with recent memories of Jack the Ripper, whose killings had terrorised Whitechapel only nine years before Stoker's book was published. Much like the Ripper, Dracula was a mysterious creature who killed by night. By connecting Dracula with this area and its most reviled criminal,

Stoker added another dimension of fear and distaste to his already ghastly villain.

✦ *Turn right on to Chicksand Street, and walk along to the junction with Brick Lane. Turn left and continue for 140 feet. Just before a decorative wire archway, you'll see a white building with a red-brick marker for the Frying Pan pub over the corner. At the time of writing it is the Brick Lane Hotel.*

The Frying Pan pub was the last place where another Ripper victim Mary Ann Nichols – also known as Polly – was seen alive. She appears as 'Polly' at the beginning of *A Study in Terror*, drinking in the pub with one of her clients. When her client catches her stealing, she loses her fee for the night and is forced out onto the dangerous streets. In Bob Clark's later Holmes/Ripper crossover, *Murder By Decree*, Polly Nichols plays a role in Dr John Watson's investigations. Watson poses as a journalist reporting on Polly's death, as a cover for his investigation of the Whitechapel murders. Feigning a deep interest in Polly and her personal life, Watson gains the sympathy of some of Polly's acquaintances who reveal she is a close friend of Mary Kelly. Later, Holmes realises that Mary Kelly is the intended Ripper victim, and that Polly was killed because Mary shared a vital secret with her.

In *From Hell*, Polly is the sex worker that Jack the Ripper takes to see the sight of Cleopatra's Needle, described in the Covent Garden walk. To summarise, in the film the Ripper picks her up from outside the Ten Bells, rather than this pub, and after strangling her at the Needle, returns to Buck's Row in the East End (the actual place Polly's body was found) to mutilate her body. As with much of the film, CGI was used to turn a street in Prague into a recreation Buck's Row, including the then cobbled streets. On the way to the next stop we pass Buck's Row, now called Durward Street, on your left.

✦ *Continue south along Brick Lane, which becomes Osborn Street, to the junction with Whitechapel High Street / Whitechapel Road.*

We are moving from Spitalfields into Whitechapel, where more of the Ripper victims were killed. Whitechapel is also the main location for Gerard Kikoine's Jekyll and Hyde horror *Edge of Sanity* (1989) in which Dr Jekyll's experiments with mind altering drugs release his supressed childhood trauma in the violent persona of Hyde. In this telling of the story, Hyde travels to Whitechapel to visit an underground club, where he drugs an exotic dancer and one of the club's male workers to perform in Hyde's sadomasochistic fantasies. The film is surreal: set largely in the Victorian era, the club scenes bizarrely mimic eighties interior design and costuming, making the scenes in Whitechapel seem uncannily modern. Most of the film was filmed in Hungary but the director included Whitechapel's back alleys to establish a parallel between Hyde's violence on sex workers with the Ripper murders.

If you look left along Whitechapel Road you can see the road bend toward the Royal London Hospital, opposite Whitechapel Station. The Hospital was founded in the 18th century as a voluntary infirmary offering free medical care to people of London who could not afford it. Included among its former patients is John Merrick, known as 'The Elephant Man', and perhaps best remembered from John Hurt's moving performance in David Lynch's *The Elephant Man* (1980).

Born in Leicester in 1862, Merrick developed bodily and facial malformation at an early age. At 17 he decided to earn extra money exhibiting his unique features as a spectacle in a shop in Whitechapel and later joined freakshows and circuses, even travelling to Europe. Though he made some money, when the industry waned, he returned to London nearly penniless. While being shown in Whitechapel, relatively near the Royal Hospital, he came to the attention of Dr Frederick Treves who later saved Merrick from his impoverished life and took him to the Royal London as a resident. Treves treated Merrick, managing his pain and arranging for Merrick to make visits outside the hospital to theatres and the countryside. Merrick died in relative comfort under Treves' care, and his remains are still preserved in the hospital as part of its teaching collection.

Merrick's time at the hospital is referenced in a brief scene in *From Hell* in which he is unveiled to a shocked crowd of doctors, including the Queen's physician, Dr William Gull. The spectacle and treatment of Merrick in the scene is meant to demonstrate how inhumane and callous the doctors are, laying the groundwork for Inspector Abberline's discovery that these Freemason-doctors arranged and covered up the macabre Ripper murders. It should be said that this representation doesn't fit with the more convivial reality of Treves' documented relationship with his patient.

✦ *Cross Whitechapel High Street / Whitechapel Road by the pedestrian crossing to your left. White Church Lane runs along the right hand side of Altab Ali Park; walk down here to the junction with Commercial Road. Turn left and follow Commercial Road for 175 yards to the junction with Henriques Street. Turn right and walk down to an archway marked 'Boys' – once the entrance to a school, and before that known as Dutfield's Yard.*

The third murder victim of Jack the Ripper, Elizabeth Stride, was discovered here at Dutfield's Yard on what used to be called Berner Street. As one of the 'middle murders' in the Ripper's series of crimes, Stride's death is sometimes overlooked. But there is however a Ripper theory that his victims' bodies were arranged to mimic the form of a pentacle as a symbol of the Masons and their power over the city. This theory is alluded to in *From Hell* when Dr Gull goes mad with power insisting that he is the embodiment of the energy at the heart of London, an energy concentrated and conveyed by symbols like the pentacle star.

This exact location has not been replicated in horror films, but Elizabeth Stride is a minor presence in *A Study in Terror, Murder By Decree* and the 1988 *Jack the Ripper*. She also makes an important if unusual appearance in Peter Sasdy's *Hands of the Ripper* (1971). This film tells the story of Anna, the daughter of Jack the Ripper who falls into unexpected trances in which she kills people. Anna is taken into the care of psychologist, Dr Pritchard, but he is unable to control her outbursts and she kills several people, including a sex worker known as 'Long Liz'. This was the popular nickname of Elizabeth Stride. Her appearance is quixotic, as Anna's father should have already killed Long Liz. Anna encounters Liz here on Berner Street in the film. As you can see, the street was subsequently renamed Henriques Street, but *Hands of the Ripper* keeps the Victorian Street name for an eerie reproduction of Long Liz's murder. This doubling is a surreal tip of the hat to the original Ripper murders, demonstrating perhaps how closely Anna is reliving her father's horrific deeds.

✦ *Continue along Henriques Street to the junction with Fairclough Street. Turn right and walk along to the junction with Back Church Lane. Turn left and follow Back Church Lane to the junction with Cable Street. Cross Cable Street, turn right, and walk along to the junction with Ensign Street. Turn left, then take another immediate left on to Graces Alley. Walk along to Wilton's Music Hall – look out for the arched red door with stone floral decorations on either side.*

Wilton's is one of the oldest surviving music halls in London. Both inside and out it is a unique example of restoration, leaving a sense of the distant past and the Gothic lingering in the modern East End. The atmosphere makes it a popular venue to visit and to film.

In Oliver Parker's horror remake of *Dorian Gray* (2009), you can see Wilton's in its Victorian setting, as this is the theatre where Dorian meets his first love, the actress Sybil. Dorian takes Lord Henry to see Sybil perform at the hall, and in the scene you can see Dorian watching the stage from behind one of the theatre's unique spiral-carved pillars while his friend watches from above. The two men linger after the performance so that Lord Henry can meet Sibyl once the audience leaves, and though Sibyl is kind and sweet, Lord Henry discreetly tells Dorian that he should not waste marriage on an impoverished actress. The moment is the start of Dorian's downfall – he decides to break up with Sybil to live up to Lord Henry's expectations, only for Sybil to throw herself into the Thames. This sends Dorian spiralling into drug addicted depression and also marks the first moment the story's legendary painting takes on the stress and pain of Dorian's soul.

The other horror connection of Wilton's is Peter Ackroyd's novel *Dan Leno and the Limehouse Golem* (1994), adapted for film as *The Limehouse Golem* by Juan Carlos Medina in 2016. In Ackroyd's novel, Wilton's is one of the many music halls mentioned by Elizbeth Cree and Dan Leto as they tour with their various acts. Wilton's certainly is the best London opportunity to see the Music Halls that are the focus of Ackroyd's book, but film buffs will have to go to Dalton Mills in West Yorkshire to see the filming location on which they built the stage for the 2016 film.

In another near-miss of horror film history, it is a popular belief that Neil Jordan's romantic vampire horror *An Interview with the Vampire* includes shots of Wilton's Music hall (it is even now listed as a location on IMDB!). Wilton's, though, will be the first to say no filming was done in the theatre for that particular movie. The most popular claim is that the grand guignol scenes were shot here. Those scenes were actually shot on set, but the aged design does resemble Wilton's unique decayed and Gothic feel. You can experience the atmosphere for yourself by getting a ticket for any of the shows and concerts held at Wilton's throughout the year.

✦ *Retrace your steps along Graces Alley to Ensign Street. Turn left, and walk down Ensign Street to the junction with the wide and busy Highway. Turn right and follow the Highway, then East Smithfield, for a quarter of a mile to a large and busy crossroads, with the Tower of London visible on the far side. Cross the road directly ahead of you, then take a footpath that leads down a flight of stairs and along the north side of the Tower.*

If you've followed the Thames walk in this book, you'll recognise this as a location from Peter Sykes' 1974 film adaptation of Dennis Wheatley's *To The Devil ... A Daughter*. Along this northern path the nun Catherine

flees under the telepathic power of defrocked priest
Father Michael, played by Christopher Lee. On this walk,
though, we'll end more appropriately by reflecting on
the Tower's relationship to the East End.

The Tower of London, and Tower Bridge beyond, are
part of the concluding moments of Matthias Hoene's
unique East End horror film, *Cockneys vs Zombies* (2012).
Unlike the other films on this walk, *Cockneys vs Zombies*
does not include a wisp of fog or a single gas lamp. But
even though it is set in the contemporary East End, the
area's past is crucial to the story. The title gives away the
important historical link: Cockneys have been around
much longer than the Ripper, and the term has been
used to refer to a native Londoner since as early as 1600.
According to the traditional definition, a Cockney had to
be born within earshot of the bells of St Mary-le-Bow's
church in Cheapside, but today it reflects an inherited
sense of belonging to the working-class East End.

The importance of being a Cockney, and the strength
it gives to London, is celebrated in the final scene of
the film as a group of survivors float by the Tower of
London. Once the band of family and friends escape the
land-bound zombies on the waters of the Thames, they
worry about London's ability to survive this new foe. The
grandfather Ray – who is played by Alan Ford, famous
for portraying a Cockney in Guy Ritchie's East End films
– assures them that if the military can't solve the zombie
invasion he will 'round up every nutter' in the East End
and they can defeat the zombies themselves. The spirit
of the Cockney people is all Ray needs to feel assured

London can survive. In these final moments, as in all the films of this walk, the past defines the East End, even when looking to its future.

Looking for More?

Most horror films set in the East End are set in the Victorian era, making the most of the neighbourhood's connection to Jack the Ripper. But as much as the East End is defined by this Gothic image, there are many other Gothic and Victorian film locations throughout the city, including these horror hotspots:

Mary-le-Bow Church

Transport: Mansion House
Underground Station
(.1 miles)

Bank Underground and
Overground Station (.2 miles)

If you were inspired by Ray's riveting speech at the end of *Cockneys vs Zombies*, then head straight to Mary-le-Bow Church. To be Cockney was once strictly defined as being born within hearing distance of this church's bells. Given that the church is in the heart of the City of London, we have to imagine how quiet the city must have been for people two miles away in Whitechapel to hear the 'Bow Bells' ring. The Bow Bells is also the name of a care home in *Cockneys vs Zombies*, in a nod to this church and its history. In many of the films along these walks, you might have noticed that Cockneys are usually the victims, or minor characters in films, and the heroes have a smoother accent and higher social status. *Cockneys vs Zombies* upended this tradition by combining the bloke-horror-hero storyline of *Shaun of the Dead* with the East End gangster films of Guy Ritchie.

Beyond its on-screen appearances, the church is rumoured to have occult connections reaching back almost a thousand years. In the 11th and 12th centuries, black masses were reputedly held in the crypt, drawing a curse down upon the church. Whatever the truth of these claims, the church seems to have suffered a remarkable run of bad luck. The roof blew off in 1091; the church caught fire in 1196 after the Bishop of London tried to smoke out a criminal claiming sanctuary; another criminal, Laurence Duket, was murdered in the church in the 13th century; the tower collapsed in 1271, crushing members of the congregation at prayer; and the entire church was destroyed along with much of the city in the Great Fire of 1666. The rebuilt church – one of Christopher Wren's most lively designs – has led a more tranquil existence; perhaps Wren used Masonic ritual and design to lift the curse?

Old Royal Naval College, Greenwich

Transport: Cutty Sark DLR   Maze Hill Rail Station
Station (.2 miles)   (.5 miles)

Also designed by Christopher Wren and protected as a UNESCO heritage site, the Old Royal Naval College is frozen in time, making it an ideal historical London setting for a film, horror or otherwise. Despite being built over the seventeenth and eighteenth centuries, the area is often used in horror as a Victorian backdrop, and rarely plays a college on screen. In Stephen Sommers' *The Mummy Returns* (2001), the Royal Naval College stands in for London streets during a chase scene where mummies attack explorer Rick as he attempts to escape on a London bus (also mentioned on the Bloomsbury walk). We see the same generic use of the college in the 2009 *Dorian Gray*, where the buildings provide a background for Dorian's nocturnal wanderings, and again in Joe Johnston's *The Wolfman* (2010) as the police chase werewolf Lawrence Talbot through the streets of London – in fact, filmed along four of the roads around the College.

The buildings and roads appear several times in *Murder By Decree*, starting out as a series of generic

London roads down which the medium, Robert Lees, follows physician and Freemason, Sir Thomas Spivey. Lees is helping Holmes and Watson uncover the perpetrator of the Ripper murders, and his visions lead him to suspect the well-connected Spivey. As he follows Spivey through the streets, Lees tries to explain to a police officer that Spivey is the infamous killer, only to be dismissed and asked to stop following the gentleman. Later in the film, when Watson is released from prison in the East End, the buildings behind Watson and Holmes are the northern buildings of the Royal Naval College, and a similar shot is used to show them going to the train station in another scene.

Beyond the Royal Naval College, Greenwich is worth exploring for its history, its natural beauty, and its Fortean and horror-film connections. Among the most famous supernatural sites are the haunted Tulip Staircase in the Queen's House and the marvellous Trafalgar Pub, said to be haunted by both a large black hound and a friendly gentleman wandering the upper halls. It is also the central location for Dr Orloff's murderous rampages in Walter Summers' *The Dark Eyes of London* (1939), though most of it was filmed on set. The backstreets of Greenwich were used in Robert Pratten's *London Voodoo* (2004), in which a family discover a voodoo burial beneath their house and the wife becomes possessed. The film was (perhaps tastelessly) inspired by the discovery of a torso floating in the Thames in 2001 which belonged to an African boy. There is still no official verdict on the death of the child, or certainty around his identity, but his body is assumed to have been part of a ritual sacrifice since 2002 when a witness came forward with information about child trafficking for use in rituals.

Madame Tussauds Wax Museum

Transport: Baker Street
Underground Station
(.1 mile)

Regent's Park Underground
Station (.3 miles)

Founded in 1835, this is surely the most uncanny mainstream museum in London, filled with lifelike replicas of the living and the dead. Throw in the museum's notorious 'Chambers of Horrors' and you get the inspiration for Walter Summers' silent *Chamber of Horrors* (1929), in which the boastful James spends the night in the Chamber with – of course – horrific consequences. Using the same plot device, George Pearson's *Midnight at Madame Tussaud's* (1936) puts a screenplay writer in the wax museum overnight, unexpectedly placing himself and his ward in danger. *Midnight in Madame Tussaud's* was, rather splendidly, filmed inside the museum after hours, giving the movie a disturbing reality while teasing out the eerie nature of the wax models.

And yet, the figures are not always a source of terror. In W. Lee Wilder and Charles Saunders' *The Man Without A Body* (1957) dying millionaire Karl Brussard visits Madame Tussauds for inspiration while finding a brain to transplant into his body. Among the figures, he decides that his new brain will be that of the 16th century astrologer Nostradamus, and catches a flight to France to do a spot of graverobbing. The rest of his story is told in the Harley Street hotspot.

As its title suggests, Charles Lamont's *Abbott and Costello meet Dr Jekyll and Mr Hyde* (1953) manages to wring comedy out of the museum's Chamber of Horrors. Two hapless cops, Tubby and Slim, are fired for incompetence and try to win their jobs back by tracking down a mysterious serial killer in the heart of London. Investigating the crime, Tubby discovers a werewolf version of Dr Hyde and chases him into the museum. The wax scares Tubby more than the audience, and he jumps at the sight of some of the statues in a fake torture chamber, nearly losing the werewolf. Out of sheer luck, Tubby manages to trap the wolf/Hyde in one of the exhibit's prison cells and goes to tell the chief of police. By the time Tubby returns with his former boss in tow, the cell contains the respected physician Dr Jekyll. Not suspecting the transformation, the police chief releases Jekyll with abundant apologies – but for a moment Tubby had saved the day, trapping a real murderer in Madame Tussauds.

Filmography

Here you can find the films referenced in the walks and horror hotspots, including a few non-horror films. As I said in the introduction, this is not a definitive list of every horror film shot in London, but these films capture horror cinema's most frequented and inspiring London locations. The synopses include which walks or hotspots the films featured in to give you a taste of how the film showcased London.

10 *Rillington Place* (1971, dir. Richard Fleischer)

When Beryl's pregnancy puts a strain on her finances and marriage to Timothy, she turns to her neighbour, John Christie, for help, unaware that Christie is a serial killer. Based on a true story. Starring Richard Attenborough as John Christie, Judy Geeson as Beryl, and John Hurt as Timothy. Featured in the '10 Rillington Place' hotspot.

28 *Days Later* (2001, dir. Danny Boyle)

Bike messenger Jim awakes from a coma to London desolated by the Rage virus. He and fellow survivors, Selena and Hannah, seek safety and other survivors while avoiding roving bands of Rage-infected cannibals. Starring Cillian Murphy as Jim and Naomie Harris as Selena. In the Westminster, Bloomsbury, London Underground, and Thames walks.

28 *Weeks Later* (2007, dir. Juan Carlos Fresnadillo)

Tammy and Andy reunite with their father in quarantined London, but when they break the army's restrictions, they discover a secret that brings the virus back with them. Starring Imogen Poots as Tammy, Mackintosh Muggleton as Andy, Jeremy Renner as Doyle, and Rose Byrne as Scarlet. Sequel to 28 *Days Later*. In the Covent Garden and Leicester Square,

London Underground, and
Thames walks and Old
Aldwych Station hotspot.

Abbott and Costello Meet Dr Jekyll and Mr Hyde (1953, dir. Charles Lamont)

When two American police
officers – Slim and Tubby –
lose their jobs on the London
beat, they attempt to regain
employment by catching the
elusive serial killer known as
Hyde. Starring Bud Abbott as
Slim, Lou Costello as Tubby
and Boris Karloff as Dr Jekyll/
Mr Hyde. Featured in the
Madame Tussauds hotspot.

The Abominable Dr Phibes (1971, dir. Robert Fuest)

A series of baffling deaths
inspired by the ten plagues
of Egypt are seemingly tied
to the fatal car crash of noted
organist Dr Phibes and his
wife. Starring Vincent Price
as Dr Phibes. Featured in the
Highgate Cemetery hotspot.

An American Werewolf in London (1981, dir. John Landis)

Friends David and Jack are
victims of an animal attack
while backpacking in Yorkshire.
Jack dies, but appears in
visions to David as he
recovers, desperately trying
to convince David that he has
become a werewolf and is
killing people across London.
Starring David Naughton as
David Kessler, and Griffin
Dunne as Jack. In the Covent
Garden and Leicester Square
walk and the London Zoo
hotspot, Westminster
walk , Bloomsbury walk,
Thames walk, and the
Piccadilly Circus hotspot.

The Awakening (1980, dir. Mike Newell)

The cursed tomb of Queen
Kara is discovered in Egypt
and brought to London
by archaeologist Matthew
Corbeck. Corbeck attempts to
reawaken the mummy, putting
the lives of those closest to
him at risk. Based on The
Jewel of the Seven Stars by
Bram Stoker. Starring Charlton

Heston as Matthew Corbeck. In the Bloomsbury walk.

Bedlam (1946, dir. Mark Robson)

George Sims, master of the Bethlem Royal Hospital – Bedlam – will use any means necessary to hide the mistreatment within the asylum from Nell, his protege who becomes upset by the death of one of the hospital's inmates. Staring Boris Karloff as Master George Sims, and Anna Lee as Nell Bowen. Featured in the Imperial War Museum hotspot.

Behemoth the Sea Monster (1959, dir. Eugène Lourié)

A gigantic sea monster is discovered in the Irish Sea, but the British Army fails to keep the monster from attacking London, leaving the fate of the city in the hands of scientists James Bickford and Steve Karnes. Starring André Morell as Prof. James Bickford, and Gene Evans as Steve Karnes. In the Westminster and Thames walks.

Blood From the Mummy's Tomb (1971, dir. Seth Holt)

A group of nineteenth-century archaeologists discover the cursed tomb of the Egyptian queen Tera. Back in London eighteen years later, the leader of the expedition, Professor Fuchs, becomes obsessed with Tera as his daughter, Margaret, turns eighteen. Also based on Bram Stoker's *The Jewel of the Seven Stars*. Starring Andrew Keir as Professor Fuchs and Valerie Leon as Margaret. Featured in the Bloomsbury walk.

The Body Beneath (1970, dir. Andy Milligan)

When the ancient Ford family of vampires find their numbers dwindling, Reverend Alexander Ford seeks fresh blood from their distant relatives. Starring Gavin Reed as Rev. Ford and Jackie Skarvellis as Susan Ford. Featured in the Highgate Cemetery hotspot.

Bram Stoker's Dracula (1992, dir. Francis Ford Coppola)

Solicitor Jonathan Harker is imprisoned in the castle

of the mysterious Count Dracula, who has his sights set on London and Harker's beautiful fiancée, Mina. Very loosely based on Bram Stoker's novel. Starring Gary Oldman as Count Dracula, Keanu Reeves as Jonathan Harker, and Winona Ryder as Mina. Featured in the London Zoo hotspot.

Burke and Hare (2010, dir. John Landis)

Hapless conmen Burke and Hare make money digging up cadavers and selling them to Edinburgh's medical schools, but their luck changes when Hare's wife becomes suspicious of their new wealth. Based on the true story of Burke and Hare. Starring Simon Pegg as William Burke and Andy Serkis as William Hare. Featured in the Covent Garden and Leicester Square walk.

Chamber of Horrors (1929, dir. Walter Summers)

James Budgeforth, a man cheating on his wife, spends a night in the Chamber of Horrors exhibition of Madame Tussauds and is driven mad by the nightmare he experiences. Starring Frank Stanmore as James Budgeforth. Featured in the Madame Tussauds hotspot.

Cherry Tree Lane (2010, dir. Paul Andrew Williams)

The quiet suburban home of unhappy couple Christine and Mike is invaded by a group of violent hoodlums seeking revenge on the couple's son, Sebastian. Starring Rachael Blake as Christine and Tom Butcher as Mike. Featured in the Crouch End hotspot.

Children of the Damned (1964, dir. Anton M. Leader)

When a group of supernaturally intelligent children with telekinetic powers are brought to London for examination, they escape and barricade themselves in an abandoned church. Starring Barbara Ferris as Susan Eliot, Ian Hendry as psychologist Tom Lewellin and Alan Badel as geneticist David

Neville. In the Thames walk and the Old US Embassy, Grosvenor Square hotspot.

***Circus of Fear* (1966, dir. John Llewellyn Moxey)**
After an armoured car heist ends in murder, police detective Jim Elliot's investigation leads to the travelling Barberini Circus and their masked lion-tamer, Gregor. Starring Leo Genn as Jim Elliott and Christopher Lee as Gregor. Featured in the Thames walk.

***A Clockwork Orange* (1971, dir. Stanley Kubrick)**
Young sociopath Alex is arrested after a particularly aggressive assault and undergoes experimental brainwashing to cure him of his criminal desires. Based on the novel by Anthony Burgess. Starring Malcolm McDowell as Alex. Featured on the Chelsea walk.

***Close Your Eyes* (2002, dir. Nick Willing)**
Hypnotherapist Michael Strother gets caught up in the chase for a supernatural serial killer while he tries to decipher the telepathic visions of his patient, police officer Janet Losey. Based on the novel *Dr Sleep* by Madison Smartt Bell. Starring Goran Višnjić as Dr Michael Strother and Shirley Henderson as Janet Losey. In the Thames walk, and East Finchley Station hotspot.

***Cockneys vs Zombies* (2012, dir. Matthias Hoene)**
During a zombie invasion two cockney brothers, Terry and Andy, risk everything to save their grandfather, Ray, and his fellow pensioners trapped in a retirement home. Starring Rasmus Hardiker as Terry, Harry Treadaway as Andy, and Alan Ford as Ray. In the Thames and East End walks, and the Mary-le-Bow Church hotspot.

***The Conjuring 2: The Enfield Case* (2012, dir. James Wan)**
Demonologists Ed and Lorraine Warren travel to London to investigate a poltergeist menacing a family in Enfield. Based on the real case of the

Enfield Poltergeist. Starring Patrick Wilson as Ed Warren, and Vera Farmiga as Lorraine Warren. In the Enfield walk and Marylebone Station hotspot.

Corridors of Blood (1958, dir. Robert Day)

In the 19th century, Dr Thomas Bolton's experiments with anaesthetic lead him into the power of graverobber Resurrection Joe and his illegal trade in corpses. Starring Boris Karloff as Thomas Bolton and Christopher Lee as Resurrection Joe. In the Covent Garden, the Bloomsbury walk and Leicester Square walk and the Harley Street hotspot.

Corruption (1968, dir. Robert Hartford-Davis)

After an accident at a party leaves model Lynn Nolan horribly burned, her partner, eminent plastic surgeon John Rowan, attempts to restore her beauty using the pituitary glands of other women. Starring Peter Cushing as Sir John Rowan and Sue Lloyd as Lynn Nolan. In the Holland Park and Notting Hill walk.

Creep (2004, dir. Christopher Smith)

Trapped on the Underground in the middle of the night, party-girl Kate must fight for her life against a murderer who was raised in a secret medical facility just off the abandoned tunnels. Starring Franka Potente as Kate. In the Covent Garden and Leicester Square and London Underground walks and the Old Aldwych Station hotspot.

The Creeping Flesh (1973, dir. Freddie Francis)

Victorian scientist Emmanuel Hildern returns to London from New Guinea, bringing back bones which he believes belong to concentrated evil in the hope of curing his daughter, Penelope, of her madness. Water brings the bones back to life, and Hildern finds he has unleashed an ancient beast of pure evil. Starring Peter Cushing as Emmanuel Hildern, Lorna Heilbron as Penelope and Christopher Lee as Emmanuel's half-brother, James Hildern. Featured on the Thames walk.

The Dark Eyes of London
(1939, dir. Walter Summers)
A series of unexplained
drownings in the Thames are
revealed to be murder when
Diana, the estranged daughter
of one of the victims, comes
to London. As the police
investigate, they uncover an
unusual series of insurance
claims made by the insurance
broker Dr Orloff. Starring
Bela Lugosi as Dr Orloff and
Greta Gynt as Diana. On
the Thames walk and the
Old Royal Naval College and
Kensington Mansions hotspots.

The Day of the Triffids
(1962, dir. Steve Sekely)
After a meteor shower blinds
most of the world, the few left
with their sight intact struggle
to survive the takeover of
Earth by man-eating Triffid
plants. Naval officer Bill Masen
and student Susan leave
desolated London in search
of survivors, while biologists
on an offshore lighthouse try
to find the Triffids' weakness.
Based on the novel by John
Wyndham. Starring Howard
Keel as Bill Masen and

Janina Faye as Susan. In the
Westminster, Bloomsbury, and
Thames walks and Piccadilly
Circus, Marylebone Station
and Kew Gardens hotspots.

Death Line (1972, dir. Gary
Sherman; US title *Raw Meat*)
Students Alex and Patricia find
a man collapsed at Russell
Square Tube Station, but the
body's sudden disappearance
leads to the discovery of a
cannibal hunting people on
the Underground. Starring
David Ladd as Alex Campbell,
Sharon Gurney as Patricia,
Hugh Armstrong as Man,
and Donald Pleasence as
police Inspector Calhoun.
In the Bloomsbury, Covent
Garden and Leicester Square
and London Underground
walks and the Holborn
Police Station and Old
Aldwych Station hotspots.

The Deaths of Ian Stone
(2007, dir. Dario Piana)
Unremarkable hockey player
Ian dies suddenly in a car
accident, only to awaken in the
middle of another life. As he
lives and dies over and over

again, he comes to realise his deaths are linked to his friendship with the beautiful, kind Jenny. Starring Mike Vogel as Ian Stone and Christina Cole as Jenny. Featured on the Covent Garden and Leicester Square walk.

Devil Doll (1964, dir. Lindsay Shonteff)

Reporter Mark English and his girlfriend, Marianne, inadvertently risk their lives when they befriend The Great Vorelli – a ventriloquist with a highly unusual doll, Hugo. Starring Bryant Haliday as The Great Vorelli, William Sylvester as Mark and Yvonne Romain as Marianne. Featured in the Piccadilly Circus hotspot.

Dorian Gray (1970, dir. Massimo Dallamano)

A painting with strange powers grants Dorian eternal youth – but also pushes him into a spiral of violence, murder, and ultimately despair. Based on the novel by Oscar Wilde. Starring Helmut Berger as Dorian Gray. Featured in the Chelsea walk.

Dorian Gray (2009, dir. Oliver Parker)

Another adaptation of Wilde's novel. Starring Ben Barnes as Dorian Gray. In the East End walk and Old Royal Naval College hotspot.

Dr Jekyll and Sister Hyde (1971, dir. Roy Ward Baker)

Dr Henry Jekyll discovers that doses of female hormones will prolong his life – but with the unexpected side-effect of releasing his more confident and commanding female side, Edwina Hyde. When they run out of cadavers, Jekyll and Hyde must look elsewhere for the hormones, even if it means murder. Inspired by Robert Louis Stevenson's The Strange Case of Dr Jekyll and Mr Hyde. Starring Ralph Bates as Henry Jekyll and Martine Beswick as Edwina Hyde. Featured on the East End walk.

Dr Terror's House of Horrors (1965, dir. Freddie Francis)

In this anthology piece, five strangers in a train car have their fortune told by the enigmatic Dr Schreck, each fortune more chilling than the last. The architect will return to his Scottish home and discovers a werewolf; the second man will confront a vine in his garden that cannot be cut down; the musician will be haunted by a voodoo curse; the art critic will run an artist over with his car and be haunted by his hand; and the final man will find his new marriage plagued by a vampire. Starring Peter Cushing as Dr Schreck. Featured on the London Underground walk.

Dracula (1931, dir. Tod Browning)

The vampiric Count Dracula entraps solicitor John Renfield and moves to London to prey on the beautiful young Lucy and her friend, Mina. Their only hope lies in the ancient occult knowledge of Doctor Van Helsing. Based on Bram Stoker's novel *Dracula*. Starring Bela Lugosi as Count Dracula, Helen Chandler as Mina and Edward Van Sloan as Van Helsing. In the Westminster and Covent Garden and Leicester Square walks.

Dracula (1958, dir. Terence Fisher)

When librarian Jonathan Harker goes missing in Transylvania, Doctor Van Helsing arrives to discover Harker has been turned into a vampire by the infamous Count Dracula, and Harker's fiancée, Lucy, is mysteriously ill. Loosely based on Bram Stoker's novel. Starring Christopher Lee as Count Dracula and Peter Cushing as Van Helsing. Featured on the Bloomsbury walk.

Dracula A.D. 1972 (1972, dir. Alan Gibson)

Count Dracula is resurrected in Swinging London by hipster Johnny Alucard, who aids the Count in procuring his most precious victim: Van Helsing's great-great granddaughter, Jessica. Sequel to the 1960 film *The Brides of Dracula*. Starring Christopher Lee as Count Dracula, Peter Cushing as Lorrimer/Lawrence Van Helsing and Stephanie Beacham as Jessica Van Helsing. Featured on the Chelsea walk, the Holland Park and Notting Hill walk.

Edge of Sanity (1989, dir. Gérard Kikoïne)

As he experiments with mind-manipulating drugs, Henry Jekyll accidentally discovers a concoction which releases his unconscious mind's alter-ego, Edward Hyde. Scarred by childhood sexual torture, Hyde goes on a killing spree in London's East End. Inspired by the historical murders of Jack the Ripper and Robert Louis Stevenson's *The Strange Case of Dr Jekyll and Mr Hyde*. Starring Anthony Perkins as Dr Jekyll/Mr Hyde. Featured on the East End walk.

The Elephant Man (1980, dir. David Lynch)

Surgeon Frederick Treves discovers severely deformed John Merrick living in squalor and working in freak-shows. Treves takes Merrick to the Royal London Hospital for treatment and study. Starring Anthony Hopkins as Frederick Treves and John Hurt as John Merrick. Featured on the East End walk.

The Fiendish Plot of Dr Fu Manchu (1980, dir. Piers Haggard)

Dr Fu Manchu plans to steal a rare diamond from the Tower of London, using Queen Mary as ransom – only the police have replaced Queen Mary with policewoman Alice Rage. The final instalment of the Fu Manchu film series, inspired by the Fu Manchu novels of Arthur Henry Ward ('Sax Rohmer'). Starring Peter Sellers as Dr Fu Manchu/Sir Denis Nayland Smith and Helen Mirren as Alice Rage. In the Thames and Bloomsbury walk.

Frankenstein and the Monster from Hell (1974, dir. Terence Fisher)

After escaping a fire, Dr Victor Frankenstein reinvents himself as psychiatrist Dr Carl Victor. With the help of an asylum inmate, Simon Helder, Victor continues his work of reanimating the dead. Sequel to Hammer's 1969 *Frankenstein Must Be Destroyed* and inspired by Mary Shelley's novel. Starring

Peter Cushing as Victor Frankenstein/Carl Victor and Shane Briant as Simon Helder. Featured in the Highgate Cemetery hotspot.

Frenzy (1972, dir. Alfred Hitchcock)

When down-on-his luck barman Richard Blaney becomes the chief suspect in the Necktie Murders, he goes on the run with the help of his girlfriend Babs. Blaney and Babs place their faith in Bob Rusk – who turns out to be the wrong man to trust. Starring Jon Finch as Richard Blaney, Anna Massey as Babs Milligan and Barry Foster as Bob Rusk. In the Westminster, Covent Garden and Leicester Square, and Thames walks.

From Hell (2001, dir. Albert and Allen Hughes)

Psychic police detective Frederick Abberline takes on the case of Jack the Ripper and becomes romantically entangled with Mary Kelly, an intended victim. Inspired by the murders of Jack the Ripper and based on the graphic novel by Alan Moore. Starring Johnny Depp as Frederick Abberline and Heather Graham as Mary Kelly. In the Westminster, Bloomsbury, Covent Garden and Leicester Square, Thames and East End walks and the St Paul's Cathedral hotspot.

Full Circle (1977, dir. Richard Loncraine; US title *The Haunting of Julia*)

After the death of her daughter, Julia Lofting moves into a new home, which is haunted by the ghost of a little girl. Julia is torn between the girl's violent history while alive and her motherly instincts. Based on the novel *Julia* by Peter Straub. Starring Mia Farrow as Julia Lofting. Featured on the Holland Park, Bloomsbury and Notting Hill walks.

Gorgo (1961, dir. Eugène Lourié)

A reptilian sea monster is captured off the coast of Ireland, and brought to London as a circus attraction – but the monster's (much larger) mother returns to rescue her child. Starring Bill Travers as Captain Joe Ryan. In the Chelsea, Westminster, Covent Garden and Leicester Square, London Underground and Thames walks.

Hands of the Ripper
(1971, dir. Peter Sasdy)
Having seen her mother murdered by her father, Jack the Ripper, young Anna is severely disturbed. Psychiatrist John Pritchard takes her in, but he is unable to cure her murderous trances. Starring Angharad Rees as Anna and Eric Porter as Dr John Pritchard. Featured in the East End walk and the St Paul's Cathedral hotspot.

The Haunted House of
Horror (1969 dir. Michael
Armstrong; also titled Horror
House and The Dark)
Bored of London's party scene, a group of twenty-somethings spend the night in a supposedly haunted mansion. One of them is murdered after a seance, but none have any idea who the killer could be. Starring

Frankie Avalon as Chris and Carol Dilworth as Dorothy. Featured in the Soho hotspot.

Horrors of the Black Museum
(1959, dir. Arthur Crabtree)
Crime writer Edmond Bancroft follows a series of murders across London performed using weapons from Scotland Yard's Black Museum, which inspired Bancroft's own collection of antique torture devices which he maintains with his assistant, Rick. Starring Michael Gough as Edmond Bancroft and Graham Curnow as Rick. In the Chelsea, Holland Park and Notting Hill, and Westminster walks.

Hot Fuzz (2007, dir.
Edgar Wright)
Ambitious young police officer Nicholas Angel is disappointed with his reassignment to the sleepy town of Sandford until a series of unusual accidents lead him and his partner, PC Danny Butterman, to suspect foul play. Second in Pegg and Frost's 'Three Flavours Cornetto trilogy' of horror films. Starring Simon Pegg as

Nicholas Angel and Nick Frost as Danny Butterman. Featured on the Westminster walk.

House of Whipcord (1974, dir. Pete Walker)

After discovering her boyfriend using explicit pictures of her for his art, model Anne-Marie runs off with the eccentric Mark E. DeSade. Whe she arrives, Anne-Marie realises the estate is a torture chamber run by DeSade and his mother, Margaret. Starring Penny Irving as Anne-Marie, Robert Tayman as Mark DeSade and Barbara Markham as Margaret. Featured in the Soho hotspot.

The Hunger (1983, dir. Tony Scott)

Aging vampire Miriam seeks the help of human doctor Sarah Roberts for her lover, John, who wants to stay young. Starring Catherine Deneuve as Miriam, David Bowie as John and Susan Sarandon as Sarah. Featured in the St Paul's Cathedral hotspot.

I Don't Want to Be Born (1975, dir. Peter Sasdy; US title The Devil Within Her)

Newlyweds Lucy and Gino Carlesi bring their new-born son home to Chelsea. Lucy is afraid of the infant, though Gino and her doctor believe she has post-partum depression, and suspects her child has been cursed. Starring Joan Collins as Lucy and Ralph Bates as Gino. Featured on the Chelsea walk.

I, Monster (1971, dir. Stephen Weeks)

Psychologist Charles Marlowe is developing a drug to release inhibitions, but when he takes it himself he is transformed into the vicious and violent Edward Blake. Concerned that his client, Marlowe, is being blackmailed, lawyer Frederick Utterson decides to follow Blake. Based on Robert Louis Stevenson's *The Strange Case of Dr Jekyll and Mr Hyde*. Starring Christopher Lee as Dr Marlowe/Edward Blake and Peter Cushing as Frederick Utterson. Featured in the Kew Gardens hotspot.

Interview with the Vampire (1994, dir. Neil Jordan)
18th century plantation owner Louis struggles with his new life as a vampire under the guidance of the erratic Lestat, who will do anything – even convert an innocent child, Claudia – to keep Louis close. Starring Brad Pitt as Louis, Tom Cruise as Lestat and Kirsten Dunst as Claudia. Featured in the East Finchley hotspot.

It! (1967, dir. Herbert J. Leder; also titled *Curse of the Golem*)
After a warehouse fire the only surviving object – a statue with Hebrew engravings – arrives at the London Museum. The museum's assistant curator, Arthur Pimm, discovers the statue is a golem, and tries to command its supernatural powers. Starring Roddy McDowall as Arthur Pimm and Alan Seller as the Golem. In the Thames walk and the Imperial War Museum hotspot.

Jack the Ripper (1959, dir. Monty Berman and Robert S. Baker)
Scotland Yard Inspector O'Neill asks his friend, American detective Sam Lowry, to help him investigate a series of murders in Whitechapel. Based on the true story of Jack the Ripper. Starring Lee Patterson as Detective Sam Lowry and Eddie Byrne as Inspector O'Neill. Featured on the East End walk.

Jack The Ripper (1976, dir. Jesús Franco; original title *Der Dirnenmörder von London*)
The deranged Dr Dennis Orloff murders East End women, but accidentally leaves a witness – the blind Mr Bridger – to his crimes. Also based on the real murders of Jack the Ripper. Starring Klaus Kinski as Dr Orloff. Featured on the Chelsea walk.

Konga (1961, dir. John Lemont)
Botanist Dr Charles Decker returns from Africa with a method of growing plants and animals to enormous

size. Things go quickly wrong when he uses his experiments with the chimpanzee Konga to kill off his competition in the scientific community. Starring Michael Gough as Charles Decker and Margo Johns as his assistant, Margaret. Featured on the Westminster walk.

Last Night in Soho (2021, dir. Edgar Wright)

Fashion student and mildly psychic Eloise finds herself having vivid dreams about the woman who lived in her room in the 1960s. These dreams start as an inspiration for Eloise, who idealises the 1960s, but they soon become a nightmare as Eloise is beset by ghosts and witnesses a brutal murder. Starring Thomasin McKenzie as Eloise, Anya Taylor-Joy as Sandie and Diana Rigg as Miss Collins. Featured on the Bloomsbury walk and Piccadilly Circus and Soho hotspots.

Lifeforce (1985, dir. Tobe Hooper)

Astronaut Col. Tom Carlsen is the only survivor of a space mission in which three naked, humanoid aliens are discovered. One of the aliens, Space Girl, escapes and begins stealing the souls of humans. Carlsen, with the help of SAS colonel Colin Caine, discovers he has a psychic link to Space Girl which may help them stop her. Based on Colin Wilson's novel *The Space Vampires*. Starring Steve Railsback as Tom Carlsen, Peter Firth as Colin Caine, and Mathilda May as Space Girl. Also featuring Patrick Stewart as Dr Armstrong. In the Bloomsbury and London Underground walks and St Paul's Cathedral hotspot.

The Limehouse Golem (2016, dir. Juan Carlos Medina)

Scotland Yard detective John Kildare investigates a series of gruesome murders in Limehouse. Kildare finds evidence that the murders are linked to John Cree, whose wife Lizzie is being tried for his murder. Based on Peter Ackroyd's *Dan Leno and the Limehouse Golem*. Starring Bill Nighy as John Kildare and Olivia Cooke as Lizzie Cree. In the Bloomsbury and East End walks.

A Lizard in a Woman's Skin (1971, dir. Lucio Fulci, originally titled Una Lucertola con la Pelle di Donna)

Carol Hammond, the daughter of a British politician, dreams of her neighbour's murder. When the neighbour is killed, and Carol becomes the chief suspect, she begins to fear she is losing her mind. Starring Florinda Bolkan as Carol Hammond. Featured in the Royal Albert Hall hotspot.

The Lodger (1944, dir. John Brahm)

During a spate of murders in Whitechapel, the mysterious Mr Slade rents a room in the family home of Kitty Langley. Slade takes an interest in Kitty, but his nocturnal habits raise the suspicions of Scotland Yard detective John Warwick. Also based on Marie Belloc Lowndes' novel. Starring Merle Oberon as Kitty Langley, Laird Cregar as Mr Slade, and George Sanders

as Inspector John Warwick. Featured in the Westminster, Bloomsbury and Thames walks.

The Lodger: A Story of the London Fog (1927, dir. Alfred Hitchcock)

Slade, a quiet man of unusual habits, rents a room in the house of fashion model Daisy Bunting and her parents. As a series of murders spreads fear over London, the Buntings begin to suspect Slade is the killer. Based on the novel by Marie Belloc Lowndes. Starring Ivor Novello as Slade and June Tripp as Daisy Bunting. In the Bloomsbury, Covent Garden and Leicester Square, and Thames walks.

London After Midnight (1927, dir. Tod Browning)

Aristocrat Sir Roger Balfour is found dead in his house on the outskirts of London. The police conclude this was suicide, but when a new family moves in five years later they are frightened by what appears to be a man in a beaver hat, raising suspicions that Balfour was murdered. The full film was lost in the 1965 MGM vault fire, but Turner Classic Movies reconstructed the film in 2002 using film stills and the original script. Starring Lon Chaney as The Man in the Beaver Hat. Featured on the Westminster walk.

London Voodoo (2004, dir. Robert Pratten)

When Lincoln and Sarah Mathers move to a new home in London, they discover an unusual burial in their basement. A voodoo spirit possesses Sarah, who becomes violent and unpredictable. Starring Sara Stewart as Sarah and Doug Cockle as Lincoln. Featured on the Old Royal Naval College hotspot.

Lust for a Vampire (1971, dir. Jimmy Sangster)

Beautiful young Mircalla arrives at a finishing school, to the joy of some and the demise of others. Second instalment in the Karnstein Trilogy, all based on Sheridan Le Fanu's story 'Carmilla'. Starring Yutte Stensgaard as Mircalla/Carmilla. Featured on the Bloomsbury walk.

Madhouse (1974, dir. Jim Clark)

Horror actor Paul Toombes is recovering from a fit of madness, in which he accidentally killed his wife. His dear friend Herbert Flay convinces Toombes to return to Britain and make one last horror film. When filming begins, Toombes is again surrounded by suspicious deaths. Starring Vincent Price as Paul Toombes and Peter Cushing as Herbert Flay. Featured on the Thames walk.

Man in the Attic (1953, dir. Hugo Fregonese)

Another adaptation of Marie Belloc Lowndes' *The Lodger*, inspired by the real Ripper murders. Starring Jack Palance as Slade. Featured on the Thames walk.

The Man Who Knew Too Much (1934, dir. Alfred Hitchcock)

British couple Bob and Jill Lawrence are enjoying a holiday when they accidentally find a note – a warning that a European head of state will be assassinated at a concert in the Royal Albert Hall. When criminals learn of the discovery, they kidnap the couple's daughter to keep them from revealing what they know. Starring Leslie Banks as Bob Lawrence and Edna Best as Jill Lawrence. Featured in the Royal Albert Hall hotspot.

The Man Without A Body
(1957, dir. Charles Saunders and W. Lee Wilder; also titled *Curse of Nostradamus*)

Wealthy American businessman Karl Brussard, dying of a brain tumour, comes to Harley Street to receive a brain transplant. Dr Lew Waldenhouse and his nurse, Jean, begin to have doubts when they discover Brussard has brought them the brain of Nostradamus. Starring George Coulouris as Karl Brussard, Julia Arnall and Jean and Sheldon Lawrence as Lew. On the Westminster walk and the Harley Street and Madame Tussauds hotspots.

The Medusa Touch
(1978, dir. Jack Gold)

Psychiatrist Dr Zonfeld must come to terms with the possibility that her patient, John Morlar, is telepathically responsible for a series of catastrophes across Britain. Based on *The Medusa Touch* by Peter Van Greenaway. Starring Richard Burton as John Morlar and Lee Remick as Dr Zonfeld. On the Westminster, Holland Park and Notting Hill and Bloomsbury walks.

Midnight at Madame Tussauds
(1936, dir. George Pearson)

Explorer Sir Clive Cheyne bets his friends that he can spend the night in Madame Tussaud's supposedly haunted Chamber of Horrors. His bet leaves his young ward Carol at the mercy of a violent gang. Starring James Carew as Sir Clive Cheyne and Lucille Lisle as Carol Cheyne. Featured in the Madame Tussauds hotspot.

Mindflesh (2008, dir. Robert Pratten)

Traumatised taxi driver Chris Jackson notices a woman

recurring in his vivid but eerie fantasies. When she is revealed to be a being from another plane of existence, somehow captured by Jackson's mind, he becomes the target for inter-galactic police. Starring Peter Bramhill as Chris. Featured on the Thames walk.

The Mummy (1959, dir. Terence Fisher)

A group of archeologists led by John Banning open the tomb of princess Ananka, only to discover the scroll of life. Once the scroll is read aloud, it awakens the mummified priest Kharis, who will kill those who desecrated Ananka's tomb. Starring Peter Cushing as John Banning, Christopher Lee as Kharis / The Mummy, and Yvonne Furneaux as Ananka / Isobel Banning.

The Mummy (2017, dir. Alex Kurtzman)

US Army sergeant Nick Morton gets entangled with an ancient mummy curse when he accidentally discovers the tomb of Egyptian princess Ahmanet. A reboot of *The Mummy* franchise (see *The Mummy Returns*) starring Tom Cruise as Nick Morton, Sofia Boutella as Princess Ahmanet, and Annabelle Wallis as the archaeologist Jenny. Featured on the Westminster walk.

The Mummy Returns (2001, dir. Stephen Sommers)

Rick O'Connell, his Egyptologist wife Evelyn, and their son Alex get caught up in an attempt to resurrect ancient high priest Imhotep. Sequel to the 1999 *The Mummy* and the second film in the *Mummy* franchise. Starring Brendan Fraser as Rick, Rachel Weisz as Evelyn, and Arnold Vosloo as Imhotep. In the Bloomsbury and Thames walks and Old Royal Naval College hotspots.

Murder By Decree (1979, dir. Bob Clark)

While investigating Jack the Ripper's murders in Whitechapel, Sherlock Holmes and Dr John Watson uncover a plot implicating the highest powers in Britain. Based on *The Ripper File* by Elwyn

Jones and John Lloyd. Starring Christopher Plummer as Sherlock Holmes and James Mason as John Watson. In the Westminster, Thames and East End walks and the Old Royal Naval College hotspot.

The Mutations (1974, dir. Jack Cardiff)

Students at Imperial College are mysteriously disappearing – but a travelling circus freakshow run by the brooding Lynch, and the unorthodox botanical experiments of Professor Nolter, seem to hold the key. Starring Donald Pleasence as Professor Nolter, and Tom Baker as Lynch. In the Chelsea walk and the Royal Albert Hall hotspot.

Night After Night After Night (1969, dir. Lindsay Shonteff)

Detective Inspector Bill Rowan is pursuing a black-leather-clad serial killer who is murdering women in London. When Rowan's wife becomes one of the victims his prejudice puts cocky scofflaw, Pete, before the maniacal Judge Lomax. Starring Gilbert Wynne as Bill Rowan, Donald Sumpter as Pete and Jack May as Judge Lomax. Featured in the Soho and Holborn Police Station hotspot.

Night of the Demon (1957, dir. Jacques Tourneur; US title *Curse of the Demon*)

Shortly after a colleague of his dies in strange circumstances, American psychologist Dr John Holden arrives in London for a conference. Rumours spread that the death was the result of black magic by Dr Julian Karswell, and a hidden note indicates that Holden is next. A loose adaptation of M.R. James' short story 'Casting The Runes'. Starring Dana Andrews as John Holden and Niall MacGinnis as Julian Karswell. In the Bloomsbury and Covent Garden and Leicester Square walks.

The Omen (1976, dir. Richard Donner)

When diplomat Robert Thorn moves his family to London as an ambassador, supernatural events seem to follow his son, Damien. After a priest warns that Damien is the Antichrist, Thorn teams up with a journalist to discover the truth. The first film in *The Omen* franchise. Starring Gregory Peck as Robert Thorn and Harvey Spencer Stephens as Damien. In the All Saint's Fulham and Old US Embassy hotspots.

Omen III: The Final Conflict (1981, dir. Graham Baker)

Antichrist Damien comes to London to thwart the second coming of Christ while trying to mould the son of journalist Kate Reynolds into his disciple. The only hope for humanity lies with Father DeCarlo – the one man who knows what Damien truly is. Third film in *The Omen* franchise and a sequel to *Damien: Omen II*. Starring Sam Neill as Damien Thorn, Rossano Brazzi as Father DeCarlo and Lisa Harrow as Kate Reynolds. In the Holland Park and Notting Hill walk and Old US Embassy hotspot.

Peeping Tom (1960, dir. Michael Powell)

Socially awkward film-maker Mark struggles between the murderous obsession he executes with his camera and the genuine bond growing between him and his neighbour, Helen. Starring Carl Boehm as Mark and Anna Massey as Helen. Featured on the Bloomsbury walk.

Phantom of the Opera (1962, dir. Terence Fisher)

An unseen phantom plagues the Royal Opera House, seeking revenge on writer and producer Lord Ambrose while encouraging the talents of young soprano Christine. Based on the 1910 novel *Le Fantôme de l'Opéra* by Gaston Leroux. Starring Herbert Lom as the Phantom, Michael Gough as Lord Ambrose D'Arcy and Heather Sears as Christine. In the Covent Garden and Leicester Square and Thames walks.

*Pride and Prejudice
and Zombies* (2016,
dir. Burr Steers)
A re-imagining of Jane
Austen's *Pride and Prejudice*
in which the Bennet family
and Fitzwilliam Darcy fight
zombies to keep England
safe while courting. Starring
Lily James as Elizabeth
Bennet and Sam Riley as
Mr Darcy. Featured in the St
Paul's Cathedral hotspot.

Quatermass 2 (1957, dir.
Val Guest; also titled
Enemy from Space)
Investigating reports of a
meteor shower in the remote
Winnerden Flats, Professor
Bernard Quatermass discovers
the factory is a cover-up
for an invading alien force.
Based on the BBC serial
Quatermass II, and a sequel
to *The Quatermass Xperiment*.
Starring Brian Donlevy as
Bernard Quatermass. Featured
on the Westminster walk.

Quatermass and the Pit
(1967, dir. Roy Ward Baker)
Workers digging an extension
to the London Underground
uncover a mysterious object,
which Prof Quatermass
suspects is responsible
for supernatural events in
the area. Based on the BBC
serial, and the sequel to
Quatermass 2. Starring Andrew
Keir as Bernard Quatermass
and Barbara Shelley as his
assistant, Barbara Judd. In
the London Underground
walk and the Holland Park
and Notting Hill walk.

The Quatermass Xperiment
(1955, dir. Val Guest)
Astronaut Victor Carroon, the
only survivor of a three-man
rocket test gone wrong, has
been struck dumb by his
experiences. As Professor
Quatermass, the leader
of the space programme,
struggles to understand
what happened to his crew,
Carroon begins to mutate.
Based on the BBC serial
The Quatermass Experiment.
Starring Brian Donlevy as
Bernard Quatermass and
Richard Wordsworth as Victor
Carroon. In the Westminster
walk and London Zoo hotspot.

Reign of Fire (2002,
dir. Rob Bowman)
Britain is devastated by a
dragon invasion, sparked by
expansion work on the London
Underground, and those still
alive are scattered across the
country in hidden communes.
One survivor, Quinn, is forced
to confront his past when US
Army General Denton Van Zan
arrives at his commune to find
recruits for the war against the
dragons. Starring Christian
Bale as Quinn Abercromby
and Matthew McConaughey
as Denton Van Zan. In the
Westminster, Bloomsbury and
London Underground walks.

Repulsion (1965, dir.
Roman Polanski)
When her sister leaves
her alone for the weekend,
anxious beautician Carol's
mental state rapidly declines
as her fears of men and the
outside world invade her flat.
Starring Catherine Deneuve
as Carol. Featured in the
Kensington Mansions hotspot.

Revenge of Frankenstein
(1958, dir. Terence Fisher)
Doctor Frankenstein escapes
execution and flees to
Germany, where he continues
his reanimation experiments
under a new name. Sequel
to the 1957 *The Curse of
Frankenstein*, based on the
character from Mary Shelley's
novel. Starring Peter Cushing
as Doctor Frankenstein/Von
Stein and Francis Matthews
as Dr Hans Kleve. Featured
in the Harley Street hotspot.

The Satanic Rites of Dracula
(1973, dir. Alan Gibson)
After a series of fatal occult
incidents, Scotland Yard seek
out the help of Lorrimer Van
Helsing, who discovers a plot
to release a plague into London.
Starring Peter Cushing as
Lorrimer Van Helsing, Joanna
Lumley as Jessica Van Helsing
and Christopher Lee as Count
Dracula. In the Westminster
and Thames walks and
Royal Albert Hall hotspot.

Scream and Scream Again
(1970, dir. Gordon Hessler)
A multi-narrative story reveals
a conspiracy in which the
British government and a
totalitarian state are entangled
with a London serial killer
who drains the blood of
his victims. The ensemble
cast includes Vincent Price,
Christopher Lee, Michael
Gothard, Peter Sallis, and
Peter Cushing. Featured in the
Covent Garden, Westminster
and Leicester Square walks.

Secret Ceremony (1968,
dir. Joseph Losey)
Prostitute and grieving
mother Leonora is drawn into
the unstable life of the rich,
infantile Cenci. Starring Mia
Farrow as Cenci, Elizabeth
Taylor as Leonora and
Robert Mitchum as Albert.
Featured in the Holland
Park and Notting Hill walk.

Seven Days to Noon (1950,
dir. John and Roy Boulting)
Drama. Scientist Professor
Willington steals a nuclear
warhead and threatens
to destroy London unless

Britain ceases stockpiling
nuclear weapons. Detective
Folland does everything he
can to find Willington and
the bomb, while the country
prepares for the worst. Starring
Barry Jones as Professor
Willingdon and André
Morell as Folland. Featured
in the Westminster walk.

Shaun of the Dead (2004,
dir. Edgar Wright)
When zombies take over
London, best friends Shaun
and Ed battle through the
streets of North London to
save Shaun's mum and ex-
girlfriend and get a pint. The
first instalment in the 'Three
Flavours Cornetto' trilogy.
Starring Simon Pegg as
Shaun and Nick Frost as Ed.
In the East Finchley Station
and Crouch End hotspots.

Son of Dracula (1974,
dir. Freddie Francis)
After the death of Count
Dracula his son, Count Downe,
struggles with the decision
to take his place as the King
of Darkness, aided by his
assistant Merlin. Part music

video, part comedy-horror, the film was released alongside an album by its leading man, Harry Nilsson. Starring Harry Nilsson as Count Downe and Ringo Starr as Merlin. In the Covent Garden and Leicester Square walks and Highgate Cemetery, Soho, and Harley Street hotspots.

The Sorcerers (1967, dir. Michael Reeves)
The ageing Professor Monserrat and his wife, Estelle, invent a way to experience the minds and lives of other people. They experiment on loner Mike Roscoe, but things turn sour when Estelle becomes dangerously obsessed with the thrill she gets from entering Mike. Starring Boris Karloff as Marcus Monserrat, Catherine Lacey as Estelle and Ian Ogilvy as Mike. Featured on the Chelsea walk.

Straight On Till Morning (1972, dir. Peter Collinson)
Naïve Brenda leaves Liverpool for London in order to reinvent herself, but she becomes infatuated with the attractive but disturbed Peter. Starring Rita Tushingham as Brenda and Shane Briant as Peter. Featured on the Thames walk and Kensington Mansions hotspot.

A Study in Terror (1965, dir. James Hill)
Sherlock Holmes and Dr John Watson uncover a story of blackmail and class discrimination when Scotland Yard asks for their assistance to catch Jack the Ripper. Starring John Neville as Sherlock Holmes, and Donald Houston as John Watson. In the Thames and East End walks.

Sweeney Todd: The Demon Barber of Fleet Street (1936, dir. George King)
A barber tells his client the story of Sweeney Todd, who lured wealthy customers into his barber shop before killing them, stealing their money, and serving their bodies as meat in the neighbouring pie shop. The story is based on the 1846-47

penny dreadful *The String of Pearls*. Starring Tod Slaughter as Sweeney Todd. Featured in the Fleet Street hotspot.

Sweeney Todd: The Demon Barber of Fleet Street (2007, dir. Tim Burton)

Wronged barber Sweeney Todd returns to London to exact revenge on the duplicitous, lascivious Judge Turpin, but when Turpin slips through his fingers Todd turns his malice on the city, killing his customers and serving them up in the adoring Mrs Lovett's meat pies. Film adaptation of Stephen Sondheim and Hugh Wheeler's Tony award-winning 1979 musical, and loosely based on *The String of Pearls*. Starring Johnny Depp as Sweeney Todd, Helena Bonham Carter as Nellie Lovett and Alan Rickman as Judge Turpin. In the Thames walk and the Fleet Street hotspot.

Tale of the Mummy (1998, dir. Russell Mulcahy)

Fifty years after her grandfather died searching for Talos' cursed tomb, archaeologist Samantha brings Talos' sarcophagus to London. As the planets align, the mummy wrappings reanimate and murder people across the city drawing in police detective Riley. Starring Jason Scott Lee as Detective Riley and Louise Lombard as Samantha Turkel. Fans of Gerard Butler may enjoy his cameo role early in the film. In the Bloomsbury and London Underground walks.

Tales from the Crypt (1972, dir. Freddie Francis)

In this anthology the crypt-keeper of a graveyard shares five stories with a group of tourists visiting the catacombs, but reveals the terrible secret linking all the stories at the end. Stories were taken from the comic collections *The Vault of Horror*, *Tales from the Crypt*, and *The Haunt of Fear*. Ensemble cast includes Ralph Richardson, Joan Collins, Ian Hendry, Peter Cushing, Roy Dotrice, and Patrick Magee. Featured in the Highgate Cemetery hotspot.

Taste the Blood of Dracula
(1970, dir. Peter Sasdy)
In Victorian Britain three
gentlemen meet the enigmatic
Lord Courtley at a brothel, and
are drawn into a ceremony to
revive Count Dracula. Panicked
by the ceremony, they kill
Courtley and incite Dracula's
revenge. Starring Christopher
Lee as Dracula. Featured in the
Highgate Cemetery hotspot.

Terror **(1978, dir.
Norman J. Warren)**
Director James Garrick makes
a film about the curse put
on his family by a witch, only
for the curse to spread into
his real life, threatening him
and his cousin Ann. Starring
John Nolan as James Garrick
and Carolyn Courage as Ann.
Featured on the Holland
Park and Notting Hill walk.

Theatre of Blood **(1973,
dir. Douglas Hickox)**
After the suicide of actor
Edward Lionheart, his fiercest
critics begin to die in ways
that echo Shakespearian
scenes from Lionheart's final
season. Starring Vincent Price

as Richard Lionheart. In the
Chelsea and Thames walks.

Three Cases of Murder **(1955,
dir. David Eady, George More
O'Ferrall, and Wendy Toye)**
Mystery/Thriller. Anthology
of three stories that lead
to murder. In the first, a
museum worker enters a
picture in his gallery; in the
second, two friends fall in
love with the same woman;
and in a third – based on a
short story by W. Somerset
Maugham – a politician
seeks revenge by invading the
dreams of his opponent. Cast
includes Peter Burton, David
Horne, Maurice Kaufmann
and Orson Welles. Featured
on the Thames walk.

To The Devil ... A Daughter
(1976, dir. Peter Sykes)
Occult novelist John Verney
is charged with protecting a
young nun, Catherine, from a
Satanic plot led by a Satan-
worshipping defrocked priest,
Father Michael. Starring
Richard Widmark as John
Verney, Christopher Lee as
Father Michael and Nastassja

Kinski as Catherine. In the Thames and East End walks.

Tony (2009, dir. Gerard Johnson; US title Tony: London Serial Killer)

A glimpse into the life of Tony, an anxious, socially awkward man living on a council estate in Dalston, who happens to be a serial killer. Starring Peter Ferdinando as Tony. Featured on the Covent Garden and Leicester Square walk.

The Two Faces of Dr Jekyll (1960, dir. Terence Fisher)

Mild-mannered Dr Jekyll unleashes his devious alter-ego, Hyde, as he searches for a drug to reveal the secrets of the human mind. Hyde seeks revenge on Jekyll's wife, Kitty, for falling in love with his lascivious friend Paul. Inspired by Robert Louis Stevenson's The Strange Case of Dr Jekyll and Mr Hyde. Starring Paul Massie as Jekyll and Hyde, Dawn Addams as Kitty and Christopher Lee as Paul. Featured on the East End walk.

Vampira (1974, dir. Clive Donner)

Count Dracula, lonely in his old age, revives his long-dead love, Vampira, by collecting blood samples from a group of visiting Playboy playmates, only for the blood to transform Vampira into a contemporary African American woman. Starring David Niven as Count Dracula and Teresa Graves as Countess Vampira. In the Westminster walk and the Soho hotspot.

Vampire Diary (2006, dir. Mark James and Phil O'Shea)

While making a documentary on vampire-inspired Goths, filmmaker Holly falls in love with the distant and attractive Vicki, who claims to be a real vampire in hiding. Starring Morven Macbeth as Holly and Anna Walton as Vicki. Mentioned on the Thames walk.

The Vampire Lovers (1970, dir. Roy Ward Baker)

Strange nightmares, unexplained accidents, and shocking deaths follow a beautiful young woman, who is left at the houses of various wealthy people under different names: Mircalla and Camilla. Based on Sheridan Le Fanu's 'Carmilla', and the first instalment of the Karnstein Trilogy. Starring Ingrid Pitt as Carmilla/Mircalla and Peter Cushing as General von Spielsdorf. Mentioned on the Bloomsbury walk.

Werewolf of London (1935, dir. Stuart Walker)
After a research trip to Tibet, English botanist Wilfred Glendon is approached by a Dr Yogami, who believes that he and Glendon have been bitten by a werewolf. Yogami claims that the only cure lies in a rare plant Glendon refuses to share. Starring Henry Hull as Wilfred Glendon and Warner Oland as Dr Yogami. Featured in the London Zoo hotspot.

What Have You Done to Solange? (1972, dir. Massimo Dallamano, originally titled *Cosa avete fatto a Solange?*)
When a killer is targeting students at an all-girls Catholic school, the Italian professor, Enrico Rosseni and his wife, Herta, assist the police by looking into a secret society within their school. Starring Fabio Testi as Enrico Rosseni, Karin Baal as Herta Rosseni and Joachim Fuchsberger as Inspector Barth. Featured in the Westminster walk.

Witchfinder General (1968, dir. Michael Reeves)
Witchfinder Matthew Hopkins and his assistant John Stearne pursue their young female quarry as the English Civil War devastates the country. In the town of Brandeston Hopkins' brutal actions destroy the Lowes family and bring down the ire of Sarah Lowes' fiancé, Richard Marshall. Starring Vincent Price as Matthew Hopkins, Robert Russell as John Stearne, and Ian Ogilvy as Richard Marshall. Mentioned on the Chelsea walk.

The Wolfman (2010, dir. Joe Johnston)
Actor Lawrence Talbot returns from America to his family home in Britain after his

brother goes missing. When Lawrence is attacked by a wolf, he learns from gypsies that he has become the victim of a fatal family curse. Remake. of the 1941 film *The Wolfman*. Starring Benicio del Toro as Lawrence and Anthony Hopkins as his father, John Talbot. Featured on the Old Royal Naval College hotspot.

***The Woman in Black 2: Angel of Death* (2014, dir. Tom Harper)**
During the Blitz, schoolteacher Eve takes a group of evacuated London schoolchildren to an isolated country house. They quickly discover that the house's spectral residents don't care for newcomers. Starring Phoebe Fox as Eve. Featured on the London Underground walk.

Bibliography

Aldiss, Brian. *Dracula Unbound*. London: Grafton, 1992.

Baker, Phil. 'Secret City: Psychogeography And the End of London' in *London: From Punk to Blair*, edited by Joe Kerr and Andrew Gibson, 2nd ed., 277–91. London: Reaktion Books, 2003.

Barnett, Richard, and Mike Jay. *Medical London: Two Thousand Years of Life and Death in London*. London: Strange Attractor Press, 2008.

Beresford, Matthew. *From Demons to Dracula: The Creation of the Modern Vampire Myth*. London: Reaktion Books, 2008.

Blake, Linnie. *Wounds of Nations: Horror Cinema, Historical Trauma, and National Identity*. Manchester: Manchester University Press, 2008.

Boot, Andy. *Fragments of Fear: An Illustrated History of British Horror Films*. 3rd edition. London: Creation Books, 1999.

British Horror Cinema. Edited by Steve Chibnall and Julian Petley. Vol. 53. London: Routledge, 2002.

Brunsdon, Charlotte. *London in Cinema: The Cinematic City since 1945*. London: BFI, 2007.

Christie, Ian. 'Gothic London: Recreating the Ancient City on Screen'. *Gresham College Website*. Museum of London, 2018. https://www.gresham.ac.uk/lectures-and-events/gothic-london-ancient-city-on-screen.

Castle, Alison ed. *The Stanley Kubrick Archives*. Köln: Taschen, 2016.

Clark, John. 'The Temple of Diana' in *Interpreting Roman London: Papers in Memory of Hugh Chapman*, edited by J. Bird, M. Hassall, and H. Sheldon, 1–9. Oxford: Oxbow Books, 1996.

Conrich, Ian. 'Horrific Films and 1930s British Cinema' in *British Horror Cinema*, edited by Steve Chibnall and Julian Petley, 58–70. London: Routledge, 2002.

Cooper, Ian. *Frightmares: A History of British Horror Cinema*. Leighton Buzzard: Auteur, 2015.

Coverley, Merlin. *Occult London*. 2nd edition. Harpenden, Herts: Oldcastle Books, 2017.

Craig, Rob. *Gutter Auteur: The Films of Andy Milligan*. Jefferson, NC: McFarland & Company Inc., 2012.

Curl, James Stevens. 'The Architecture and Planning of the Nineteenth-Century Cemetery'. *Garden History* 3, no. 3 (1975): 13–41.

Das, John. 'A History of Horror with Mark Gatiss Part Two: Home Counties Horror'. United Kingdom: BBC Productions, 2010.

Dave, Paul. *Visions of England: Class and Culture in Contemporary Cinema*. Oxford: Berg, 2006.

Ellis, Bill. 'The Highgate Cemetery Vampire Hunt: The Anglo-American Connection in Satanic Cult Lore'. *Folklore* 104, no. 1–2 (1993): 13–39.

———. *Raising the Devil: Satanism and the Media*. Louisville: The University Press of Kentucky, 2000.

Farrant, David. *Beyond the Highgate Vampire: A True Case of Supernatural Occurrences and Vampirism That Centred Around London's Highgate Cemetery*, 3rd edition. London: British Psychic and Occult Society, 1997.

———. 'Ghostly Walks in Highgate' in *The Hampstead & Highgate Express*. 6 Feb, 1970, p. 26.

Fisher, Mark. *The Weird and the Eerie*. London: Repeater, 2016.

Forshaw, Barry. *British Gothic Cinema*. London: Palgrave Macmillan, 2013.

Fowler, William, and Vic Pratt. *The Body Beneath: The Flipside of British Film & Television*. London: Strange Attractor Press, 2019.

Frayling, Christopher, and Derek Towers. 'Program 1: Jekyll and Hyde'. UK: British Broadcasting Corporation, 1996.

Fryer, Ian. *British Horror Film: From the Silent to the Multiplex*. Croydon: Fonthill, 2017.

Gibson, Pamela C. 'Imaginary Landscapes, Jumbled Topographies: Cinematic London' in *London: From Punk to Blair*, edited by Joe Kerr and Andrew Gibson, 2nd ed., 321–30. London: Reaktion Books, 2012.

Gilbert, Davida, and Fiona Henderson. 'London and the Tourist Imagination' in *Imagined Londons*, edited by Pamela K. Gilbert. Albany: State University of New York Press, 2002.

Hawkes, Rebecca. 'What Did the Enfield Haunting Have to Do with Ed and Lorraine Warren?' *The Daily Telegraph*, 12 May 2015.

Hutchings, Peter. *Hammer and Beyond: The British Horror Film*. Manchester: Manchester University Press, 1993.

———. 'Horror London'. *Journal of British Cinema and Television* 6, no. 2 (2009): 190–206.

———. *The Historical Dictionary of Horror Cinema*. Plymouth: The Scarecrow Press Inc., 2008.

———. 'Uncanny Landscapes in British Film and Television'. *Visual Culture in Britain* 5, no. 2 (2004): 27–40.

Jackson, Lee. *Dirty Old London: The Victorian Fight Against Filth*. New Haven & London: Yale University Press, 2014.

James, Simon R.H. *London Film Location Guide*. London: Batsford, 2007.

———. *London Movie Guide: Walks, Tours and Locations*. 2nd edition. London: Batsford, 2011.

Jenkins, Mark Collins. *Vampire Forensics: Uncovering the Origins of an Enduring Legend*. National Geographic Society: Washington DC, 2010.

Joshi, S.T. *Unutterable Horror: A History of Supernatural Fiction Volume 2: The Twentieth and Twenty-First Centuries*. Hornsea, England: PS Publishing Ltd., 2012.

Kermode, Mark. 'A Capital Place for Panic Attacks'. *The Guardian*, 6 May 2007. https://www.theguardian.com/film/2007/may/06/features.review.

Kermode, Mark and Simon Mayo. *The Movie Doctors*. London: Canongate Press, 2016.

Leggott, James. *Contemporary British Cinema: From Heritage to Horror*. London: Wallflower Press, 2008.

Luckhurst, Roger. *The Mummy's Curse*. Oxford: Oxford University Press, 2012.

Manchester, Sean. 'The Highgate Vampire' in *The Vampire's Bedside Companion*, 67–95. London: Coronet Books, 1976.

Marriot, James, and Kim Newman. *Horror: The Definitive Guide to the Cinema of Fear*. London: André Deutsch, 2006.

Meikle, Denis. *A History of Horrors: The Rise and Fall of the House of Hammer*. London: The Scarecrow Press Inc., 2009.

Mitchell, Neil, ed. *World Film Locations: London*. Bristol: Intellect Books, 2012.

Moore, Alan, and Eddie Campbell. *From Hell and Its Companion*. Marietta, Georgia: Top Shelf Productions, 2006.

Newland, Paul. 'Shaun of the Dead and the Construction of Cult Space in Millennial London' in *London On Film*, edited by Pam Hirsh and Chris O'Rourke, 193–203. Basingstoke, Hampshire: Palgrave Macmillan, 2017.

Newman, Kim. *Nightmare Movies*. London: Bloomsbury, 2011.

———. *The BFI Companion to Horror*. London: BFI, 1996.

Penner, Jonathan, Steven Jay Schneider, and Paul Duncan, eds. *Horror Cinema*. 2nd edition. Köln: Taschen, 2012.

Perks, Marcelle. 'A Descent into the Underworld: Death Line' in *British Horror Cinema*, edited by Steve Chibnall and Julian Petley, 145–55. London: Routledge, 2002.

Pike, David L. 'London on Film and Underground'. *The London Journal* 38, no. 3 (2013): 226–44.

Pirie, David. *A Heritage of Horror: The English Gothic Cinema 1946-1972*. London: The Gordon Fraser Gallery, Ltd., 1973.

Playfair, Guy Lyon. *This House Is Haunted: The Investigation of the Enfield Poltergeist*. 2nd ed. London: Sphere, 1981.

Punter, David. *The Literature of Terror Volume 2: A History of Gothic Fictions from 1765 to the Present Day*. Essex: Pearson Education Limited, 1996.

Reeves, Tony. *Movie London: Exploring the City Film by Film*. London: Titan, 2008.

Reyes, Xavier Aldana. 'Gothic Horror Film, 1960-Present' in *The Gothic World*, 389–98. New York: Routledge, 2013.

Rigby, Jonathan. *Studies in Terror: Landmarks of Horror Cinema*. Cambridge: Signum Books, 2011.

————. *English Gothic: Classic Horror Cinema 1897-2015*. 4th edition. London: Signum Books, 2015.

Rose, James. *Beyond Hammer: British Horror Cinema Since 1970*. Leighton Buzzard: Auteur, 2009.

Sanjek, David. 'Twilight of the Monsters: The English Horror Film 1968-1975'. *Film Criticism* 16, no. Fall/Winter (1991): 111–24.

Schweitzer, Dahlia. *Going Viral: Zombies, Viruses, and the End of the World*. New Brunswick: Rutgers University Press, 2018.

Senf, Carol A. '"Dracula": Stoker's Response to the New Woman'. *Victorian Studies* 26, no. 1 (1982): 33–49.

Simpson, M.J. *Urban Terrors: New British Horror Cinema 1997-2008*. Bristol: Hemlock Books Limited, 2012.

Sobczynski, Peter. '2315 Words on "Lifeforce." Yes. "Lifeforce."' *RogerEbert.com*, 2013. https://www.rogerebert.com/far-flung-correspondents/2315-words-on-lifeforce-yes-lifeforce.

Sorensen, Colin. *London on Film: 100 Years of Filmmaking in London*. London: The White Dove Press, 1996.

Steven, Mark. *Splatter Capital: The Political Economy of Gore Films*. London: Repeater, 2017.

Stoker, Bram. *Dracula*. London: Constable & Robinson Ltd, 2012.

Sugden, Philip. *The Complete History of Jack the Ripper*. London: Hachette, 2012.

Underwood, Peter, Peter Allan, Crispin Derby, Richard Howard, Sean Manchester, James Turner, and Devendra P. Varma. *The Vampire's Bedside Companion: The Amazing World of Vampires in Fact and Fiction*. London: Coronet Books, 1976.

Walker, Johnny. *Contemporary British Horror Cinema: Industry, Genre, and Society*. Edinburgh: Edinburgh University Press, 2016.

Walkowitz, Judith R. *City of Dreadful Delight: Narratives of Sexual Danger in Late-Victorian London*. Chicago: University of Chicago Press, 1992.

Warwick, Alexandra. *Jack the Ripper: Media, Culture, History*. Manchester: Manchester University Press, 2007.

Wright, Gene. *Horrorshows: The A-to-Z of Horror in Film, TV, Radio and Theatre*. London: Facts on File Publications, 1986.

Zinoman, Jason. *Shock Value: How a Few Eccentric Outsiders Gave Us Nightmares, Conquered Hollywood and Invented Modern Horror*. London: Duckworth Overlook, 2012.

Acknowledgements

First and foremost, to Richard Barnett, for saying 'there's a book in that', for reading numerous drafts, your editorial eye, the loan of your books, and a million other small things, I am unendingly grateful. I would also like to thank to Mark and Jamie for taking a chance and putting your time, effort, and the Strange Attractor name behind this book. Jamie, I am particularly indebted to you for your encouragement and editing. It wouldn't be the same book without you. And it certainly would not be the same book without Graham Humphreys who made such a spectacular cover and Natalie Kay-Thatcher for doing the striking maps that truly bring the walks to life. Thank you both for transforming my book into a work of art. Finally, I would like to show appreciation to those who helped me shape and research this book: Robert Pratten of Zen Films, the BFI library team, Chris Sapikowski, Emily Rosendahl, and Stephanie Barbir.

Strange Attractor Press
2023